The History of the Southern Railway

Also available from Allen and Unwin

HISTORY OF THE GWR VOLS 1–3
by Peter Semmens

GREAT WESTERN SAINTS & SINNERS
by W. A. Tuplin

GREAT WESTERN STEAM
by W. A. Tuplin

MEN OF THE GREAT WESTERN
by Peter Grafton

SOUTH WEST RAILWAYMAN
by Donald King

GRAVEYARD OF STEAM
by Brian Hindley

GREAT CENTRAL STEAM
by W. A. Tuplin

HISTORY OF THE LMS VOLS 1–3
by O. S. Nock

HISTORY OF THE LNER VOLS 1–3
by Michael R. Bonavia

RAILS TO DISASTER
by Malcolm Gerard and J. A. B. Hamilton

MAUNSELL'S NELSONS
by D. W. Winkworth

MEN OF THE LNER
by Peter Grafton

ON AND OFF THE RAILS
by Sir John Elliot

PRESERVED STEAM IN BRITAIN
by Patrick B. Whitehouse

RIDDLES STANDARD TYPES IN TRAFFIC
by G. Freeman Allen

THE SCHOOLS 4–4–0S
by D. W. Winkworth

STEAM'S INDIAN SUMMER
by George Heiron and Eric Treacy

TRAINS OF THOUGHT
ed. A. W. Hobson

TRAINS TO NOWHERE
by J. A. B. Hamilton

TRAVELLING BY TRAIN IN THE EDWARDIAN AGE
by Philip Unwin

The History of the Southern Railway

Michael R. Bonavia, MA, PhD, FCIT

UNWIN HYMAN
London   Sydney

First published in Great Britain by Unwin Hyman, an imprint of Unwin
Hyman Limited, 1987

UNWIN HYMAN LIMITED
Denmark House, 37-39 Queen Elizabeth Street
London SE1 2QB
and
40 Museum Street, London WC1A 1LU

Allen & Unwin Australia Pty Ltd
8 Napier Street, North Sydney, NSW 2060, Australia

Allen & Unwin with the Port Nicholson Press
60 Cambridge Terrace, Wellington, New Zealand

British Library Cataloguing in Publication Data

Bonavia, Michael R.
    A history of Southern Railway
1. Southern Railway Company – History
1. Title
385′. 09422   HE3020.S73
ISBN 0-04-385107-X

Picture Research by Mike Esau

Set in 12 on 13 point Ehrhardt by Fotographics (Bedford) Ltd
and printed in Great Britain by Mackays of Chatham

CONTENTS

LIST OF ILLUSTRATIONS

PREFACE AND ACKNOWLEDGEMENTS

Of the four great Companies created by the Railways Act of 1921, the Southern Railway certainly came closest to realising the objectives of Sir Eric Geddes, the first Minister of Transport and sponsor of the Act. Geddes was a great believer in railway electrification, dating back to his North Eastern Railway days, when it had been intended to electrify from York to Newcastle as well as around Newcastle; and he had fought to keep control of electricity generation as a function of his new ministry. Of his four creations, only the Southern was to fulfil his hopes in that direction.

In other ways too the Southern justified the amalgamation provisions of that much-criticised Act. It emerged quite quickly as a unified business, following clear policies and rising steadily in public esteem. It was free from the rivalries and in-fighting that plagued the huge, over-centralised London Midland and Scottish; it did not suffer the acute financial difficulties of the London and North Eastern; and it was less complacent, less satisfied with traditional practices, than the Great Western.

Above all, for nearly fifteen out of the twenty-five years of its life it was lucky to be managed by the most effective, most professional railwayman of his day, Sir Herbert Walker. His contemporaries, Lord Stamp, Sir Ralph Wedgwood and Sir James Milne, had more connections with the outside world – with governments, big business, and academic circles; Walker was simply supreme in his own field, of quietly running a railway. His skill lay above all in reconciling the interests of railway users with those of his shareholders; there was no conflict between public service and private profit in his philosophy.

In writing the history of the LNER I had the advantage of having worked on that railway; in writing about the Southern I have needed, and have most generously been given, help by former Southerners. It is difficult adequately to convey how much I owe them. Sir John Elliot has allowed me to quote from some of his own eloquent writings and speeches, as well as corresponding and talking with me about many personalities. To Leslie Harrington I owe a huge debt. His superb memory for detail and his long involvement with top management, ending with his distinguished leadership of the whole of BR's shipping and international services, produced many pages of fascinating material that he has allowed me to plunder.

On the motive power side I have been given the greatest possible help from very senior retired railwaymen who kept the Southern's locomotives running in the eras of both Maunsell and Bulleid – S. C. Townroe, Gordon Nicholson and A. B. MacLeod. On operating practices, and the Southern's freight (too often overlooked), Brian Hamment-Arnold and John Rogers have written me many pages based on their own intimate experience, which have assisted in educating a non-Southerner such as myself. I was much helped by A. F. R. Carling on the complexities of the bus industry when the Southern began to invest in it.

Mr S. W. Smart, well-known as an outstanding Super-intendent of Operation during a most important period of the Southern's history, has kindly furnished me with several key documents from his own records.

My thanks are due to Mrs Payne for allowing me to quote verbatim the splendid short address given by her husband to the ship's company when he was Master of the *Maid of Orleans* immediately before taking part in the D-Day landings.

Lastly, this book would never have been completed on time without the skill and speed with which Mrs Anne Haynes has uncomplainingly deciphered my often illegible manuscripts.

M.R.B.
Haslemere,
April 1986

SOURCES

The chief primary sources for a historian of the Southern
Railway are in the Public Record Office at Kew, where records of
shareholders' meetings and Chairmen's speeches, Board and
Committee minutes and also the invaluable minutes of the
Traffic Officers' Conference are kept, together with a
miscellany of other Southern documents and engineering plans.
The parliamentary papers – most easily consulted in the
Guildhall Library – contain a great deal of relevant matter, for
example in Select Committee reports such as that in connection
with the Charing Cross bridge.

The *Southern Railway Magazine* and the *Railway Gazette* are
extremely valuable background material, and biographical
details of officers are to be found in back numbers of the *Railway
Year Book*. *Times* obituaries of Chairmen, directors and chief
officers often reveal interesting facts. The files of the *Railway
Magazine* from 1923 to 1948 are also invaluable.

Previous accounts of the Southern Railway started with an
official 'history' by C. Dendy Marshall, which devoted most of
its space to the predecessors of the Southern. Charles Klapper's
Sir Herbert Walker's Southern Railway contains much fascinating
material but it is, as its title implies, more a biography than a
Company history. An excellent source of factual data is B. K.
Cooper's *Southern Railway Handbook*; and a fine description of
Walker in action is contained in Sir John Elliot's *On and Off the
Rails*. S. C. Townroe's account of Maunsell locomotives, *The
Arthurs, Nelsons and Schools of the Southern*, is not to be missed,
though there are other numerous studies of the Southern's
locomotive history, as well as more than one biography of
Bulleid.

For the war period, reference must be made to Robert Bell's
authoritative *History of the British Railways during the War,
1939–45* and to Bernard Darwin's lively account of the Southern
during the period, *War on the Line*.

Short studies, such as Michael Robbins's excellent *The Isle of
Wight Railways*, are too numerous to list. Local history librarians

are often helpful in answering queries, such as those relating to stations. In all, there is a wealth of material available, which no one has yet exhausted.

Chapter 1

A 'DIFFERENT' RAILWAY: THE BIRTH OF THE SOUTHERN

Each of the four great systems created by the Railways Act of 1921, and which existed from 1 January 1923 until midnight on 31 December 1947, was different from the others. But the Southern Railway was especially different, not so much as the result of any deliberate refusal to join in policies agreed by the other companies but more in the circumstances – internal and external – that affected its creation.

First of all, the Southern was largely exempt from the intense competition that existed between the other three main line companies along their frontier routes – London to Scotland; London to Yorkshire, to Lancashire and the Midlands; and London to the Black Country. It was protected, if that is the right word, on its eastern and southern flanks by the sea; only along its western borders did it confront the Great Western at Exeter and Plymouth, though in general Devon and Cornwall were parcelled out in separate spheres of influence. Competitive services from London existed at smaller towns such as Yeovil, Dorchester and Barnstaple; elsewhere one railway had a clear advantage, as at Launceston and Bodmin.

Internally, the Southern enjoyed the advantage of a strong central management which was relatively free from the factions that afflicted the early years of the London Midland and Scottish. It was also the only one of the Big Four that was committed to electrification from the outset, pursuing this policy unhesitatingly throughout its life.

Lastly, starting from being the lowest of the four main lines in

1

public esteem, it steadily rose until by the date of nationalisation it had probably become the public's favourite.

Of course, there were important factors working to the Southern's advantage. It served an area of Britain that was relatively immune from the worst effects of the depression during the inter-war years in the heavy industries – coal, iron and steel, and shipbuilding in particular – which disastrously damaged the economies of South Wales, the Black Country, Lancashire and Yorkshire, west Cumberland, Northumberland and Durham, and central Scotland. None of these industrial black spots was served by the Southern.

In fact, the Southern's travel market, which it exploited to the full, was augmented by the drift of population away from the depressed north and towards the more prosperous south of England. During the period, from 1923 to 1937, while the total population of England and Wales rose from 38,403,000 to 41,031,000 – that is, by 10·7 per cent – the population of the counties chiefly served by the Southern rose proportionately more: Kent by 12·5 per cent, Surrey by 15·7 per cent, West Sussex by 13·9 per cent, East Sussex by 11·7 per cent, and Hampshire by 12·3 per cent. By contrast, the populations of various major industrial centres served by the other main line railways actually fell: Manchester by 2 per cent; Leeds by 1 per cent; Sheffield by 1 per cent; and Merthyr Tydfil by a disastrous 25 per cent.

In the west of England, the position was not quite so favourable to the Southern. Devon's population was roughly static, whereas that of Cornwall fell slightly, partly due to the decline of the tin-mining industry. However, the Southern's route mileage in Cornwall was only 66 against 268 in Devon; and its main interest in each county was the peak summer holiday traffics.

The County of London, in which the Southern had 123 route miles, and with which it was more closely involved than any of the other railways from a passenger traffic angle, showed a decrease in population of 9 per cent, but this was offset by increases in the population of Greater London and the Home Counties.

With these factors in its favour, therefore, the embryo Southern Railway was born under good auspices. While the official date of the Southern's birth is that named in the Railways Act, the beginning of 1923, the date when conception took place is less certain. It could perhaps be taken as 7 June 1920, since that was the day upon which a Cabinet meeting of the Coalition Government under David Lloyd George decided to abandon the ideas of railway nationalisation that had been under discussion during and after the end of the First World War. Alternatively, conception could be considered to have taken place on 19 August 1921, the day upon which the Railways Act received the royal assent and the outlines of the four groups were irrevocably settled.

The official birthday was 1 January 1923, when the Southern Railway was incorporated and a Board of Directors took office. But it was more nominal than real, because for a considerable time thereafter the management continued to be that of three railways, each with its own General Manager. It was not until 1 January 1924 that a single management team emerged and the Southern began to function as one railway.

The Southern, under the 1921 Act, was composed of the following undertakings:

Constituent Companies (5)
The London & South Western Railway Company
The London Brighton & South Coast Railway Company
The South Eastern Railway Company
The London Chatham & Dover Railway Company
The South Eastern & Chatham Railway Companies Managing
  Committee

Subsidiary Companies (14)
The Bridgwater Railway Company
The Brighton & Dyke Railway Company
The Freshwater Yarmouth & Newport (Isle of Wight) Railway
  Company
The Isle of Wight Central Railway Company
The Lee-on-Solent Railway Company
The London & Greenwich Railway Company
The Mid-Kent Railway (Bromley to St Mary Cray) Company
The North Cornwall Railway Company
The Plymouth & Dartmoor Railway Company

The Plymouth, Devonport & South Western Junction Railway
The Sidmouth Railway Company
The Victoria Station & Pimlico Railway Company
The Isle of Wight Railway Company
The Hayling Railways Company

It was an historical anomaly that the South Eastern & Chatham Railway was not a company on its own; its two components, so long bitterly opposing each other, had declined to merge completely and so kept their identities whilst agreeing that their two undertakings should be managed as a whole for mutual benefit by a new statutory body, the Managing Committee. Its duties involved dividing the net receipts of the combined undertaking in the proportion of 59 per cent to the South Eastern and 41 per cent to the London Chatham & Dover Company.

The subsidiary companies also contained some historical curiosities, small railways long since absorbed for all practical purposes by a larger parent but which retained a nominally independent existence.

The actual process of amalgamation and absorption was carried out, as one would expect, by hard bargaining, leading to negotiated agreements as to the amount of stock in the new Company to be issued in exchange for the securities of the Companies to be wound up. An Amalgamation Tribunal, consisting of two distinguished accountants and a leading counsel, was set up to register the agreements reached and to make an award in cases where agreement could not be reached. Towards the end of 1922 the negotiations drew to a close. On 16 November the shareholders of the LBSCR agreed terms; on 17 November the LSWR; and on 13 December the South Eastern and London Chatham & Dover proprietors – despite last-minute objections from a minority who kept alive the combative spirit of these old adversaries – followed suit. An attempt during 1922 to simplify the amalgamation process by a preliminary union of the SER and the LCDR, something that should have been done many years earlier, had failed.

Useful progress had however been made by the absorption into the LSWR of the Isle of Wight Central Railway in

4

September 1922, and of the Isle of Wight Railway in November of that year.

Some of the smaller subsidiary companies presented problems. The Lee-on-Solent Railway was bankrupt and the Southern fought, right up to the Court of Appeal, against being forced to assume its liabilities, but lost the case. The tiny Freshwater Yarmouth & Newport Railway tried to increase its compensation by arguing that if a proposal for a Solent tunnel (described in Chapter 14) were to materialise it would become the main gateway by rail from the mainland to the island. This ingenious ploy carried little weight – the railway was already in the hands of a receiver – but it went on fighting for better terms until the Amalgamation Tribunal made an award in June 1923.

It should also be mentioned that soon after incorporation the Southern in 1923 obtained powers to take over the Lynton & Barnstaple Railway, a narrow-gauge (1ft 11½in.) line just under 20 miles long with four locomotives, the price paid being £39,267. More significantly, powers were taken jointly with the London Midland & Scottish Railway Company to absorb into the two parent companies' ownership the Somerset & Dorset Joint Railway, formerly leased to the Midland and London & South Western Railways. With all these moves, the Southern Railway Company was at last firmly established.

The terms agreed for the main constituent companies were designed to provide for the holders of Debentures, Preference and Preferred Ordinary stocks, those carrying a fixed rate of return, the same income from the Southern Railway as they had enjoyed from the LSWR, the LBSCR and the SER. But there was an exception – the less fortunate holders of LCDR. Preference stocks, whose dividends had been paid only irregularly (there had never been any Ordinary stock dividends), received an allocation of 'A' Ordinary shares in the Southern Railway, with no guaranteed minimum dividend.

The compensation terms for Ordinary shareholders reflected the degree of prosperity of the constituents, with the LSWR in the lead (it had paid 6 per cent on average for a long time), the Brighton next and the SER third.

The new company had a total issued capital of £144,840,215 divided in the following proportions:

	£	% of total
Loans and debentures	35,721,229	24·7
Preference stocks	45,853,878	31·6
Ordinary stocks	63,265,108	43·7
	£144,840,215	100·0

Next in importance to the terms of amalgamation came the composition of the new Board of Directors. The Railways Act had laid down in its second schedule that the 'Southern Group' Board should consist of not more than 21 Directors, all to be appointed by the constituent companies at the outset. As the result of some horse-trading, it was agreed that the first Board should be composed of eight Directors from the LSWR, five from the LBSCR, five from the SER and three from the LCDR. Two of the Chairmen – Cosmo Bonsor of the South Eastern and Sir William Hart Dyke of the Chatham – decided to retire. Cosmo Bonsor (to be knighted in 1925 as Sir (Henry) Cosmo (Orme) Bonsor) was the doyen of the Chairmen. He had first been elected to that position on the SER in 1898 and had been effectively in charge of the SECR as Chairman of the Managing Committee ever since 1899. He was now seventy-five and ready for retirement. Sir William Hart Dyke had led the Chatham Company since 1908, but the real power had obviously rested with Cosmo Bonsor. Sir William had had a distinguished political career, but was now ten years older than Cosmo Bonsor and even readier for retirement.

The Brighton chairmanship had changed hands at the last minute; Charles C. Macrae, suffering from some ill health late in 1922, had resigned and had been succeeded by Gerald W. E. Loder, who therefore, though aged sixty-two, had to be considered comparatively junior among the Chairmen (later, as Lord Wakehurst, he was to become Chairman of the Southern). Accordingly the way was clear for Brigadier-General Sir Hugh Drummond (aged sixty-four), Chairman of the LSWR since 1911, to head the new Company.

The new Board gained some other distinguished figures from the old companies. The South Eastern contributed Brigadier-General the Hon. Everard Baring, who became Deputy Chairman of the Southern and after only 19 months was to succeed Drummond as Chairman. The SER also provided a

6

remarkable personality in Charles Sheath, who had joined the South Eastern Railway when Samuel Smiles, of *Self Help* fame, had been Company Secretary. He had become Secretary himself in 1898 and in 1922 considered applying for the same post on the Southern Railway, at the age of eighty! Cosmo Bonsor dissuaded him from this and instead had him appointed a Director of the SER, from which he was nominated to the new Southern Board.

From the Brighton came F. Dudley Docker, the influential Midlands industrialist and financier. Sir Robert Turnbull, a retired General Manager of the London and North Western, brought railway expertise to the new Board, as did Sir Francis Dent from the Chatham Board: he had been General Manager of the SECR from 1911 to 1920.

The London and South Western, the largest contingent, contributed another future Southern Chairman, Robert Holland Martin. Also bringing in railway expertise was Sir Charles Owens, who had been the General Manager at Waterloo from 1898 until Walker succeeded him in 1912.

All in all, this could be considered a formidable Board, and not one to be dominated by any management it chose to appoint. However, the Chairman had for over ten years established a firm working relationship with the outstanding railway manager of his generation. Herbert Ashcombe Walker had come from the London and North Western Railway in 1912 to be General Manager of the LSWR, in which post he had so distinguished himself that upon the outbreak of war in 1914 he was appointed acting Chairman of the Railway Executive Committee. The President of the Board of Trade was the purely nominal chairman of that body, which directed the railways in all matters relating to the war effort. Walker's leadership of the other General Managers had been outstanding and led to his receiving a knighthood in the New Year Honours List of 1915 and a KCB in 1917.

Establishment of the general management was not so easy as establishing the chairmanship. Initially, the Board appointed three General Managers, those from the three constituent systems. The complications this produced and the solution that had to be found are described in Chapter 3.

7

The railway that emerged from this period of negotiation and reorganisation was considerably the smallest of the four grouped Companies. It had just under 40 per cent of the issued capital of the largest company, the LMS. It had 2,153 route-miles open for traffic against the 6,911 of the LMS. A few index numbers show the relative positions in more detail.

	SR	*GWR*	*LNER*	*LMS*
Steam locomotives	21·9	38·3	71·8	100·0
Passenger carriages	38·0	34·4	72·8	100·0
Wagons	11·7	28·2	93·3	100·0
Passenger receipts	56·9	40·8	67·3	100·0
Freight receipts (excluding coal, etc.)	14·4	33·3	65·9	100·0
Coal, etc., receipts	12·1	42·4	77·3	100·0
Staff employed	25·7	42·7	75·6	100·0

These figures demonstrate the Southern's overwhelming dependence upon passenger traffic, whereas the other three Companies relied upon freight as much as, or more than, passenger traffic. With just a quarter of the staff of the LMS, the Southern had well over half that company's passenger traffic, but less than one-sixth its freight traffic. During its lifetime, the Southern Railway generally drew about three-quarters of its gross traffic receipts from the passenger business.

The Southern's 'different' character can well be illustrated by pointing out that there were no less than 23 racecourses on the system; that it served Naval depots at Chatham, Sheerness, Dover, Portsmouth, Portland and Devonport, and Army and Air Force depots that included Aldershot, Salisbury Plain, Manston and Farnborough. All these generated special flows of traffic, as of course did the great holiday movements to the south coast, and the daily flood of commuters into and out of London on the greatest suburban railway network in the world.

Was the Southern a logically designed system? The amalgamations under the Railways Act seemed to reflect several different principles. One was longitudinal or 'end-on' amalgamation, designed to promote through running and to simplify operating and administrative procedures. Another was 'parallel' amalgamation, presumably intended to effect rationalisation, to economise by reducing competitive or duplicate services. Yet another was to bring together railways whose routes spread out from a single centre like the fingers of a hand.

The Southern may be considered to have emerged as a result of the last two principles. The cat's-cradle of lines in the south of London certainly suggested some need for rationalisation. The worst case of mutually damaging competition, however, between the South Eastern and the London Chatham & Dover, had already been dealt with when in 1899 the two railways had formed their working union. Nevertheless, the Southern did evolve an individual style of management cutting right across its old Company frontiers, in the course of a decade and a half of striking progress, due above all to the leadership of a great General Manager, Sir Herbert Walker.

Chapter 2

THE CONSTITUENTS

The London & South Western

Of the three major railways grouped in the Southern, the London & South Western had by far the best claim to be considered a major trunk line. It had come a long way since the promoters of the London & Southampton Railway had argued that it would need only *five* locomotives, and a critic had suggested that its traffic would be limited to 'parsons and prawns' – the former from Winchester and the latter from Southampton. Its main line now stretched from Waterloo for 261 miles into north Cornwall. It had London's biggest passenger terminal station, as well as the most modern freight marshalling yard in the metropolitan area, at Feltham. It handled not merely a very large suburban traffic which it had begun to carry in electric trains, but many other important traffics, especially those for the Service Departments, already mentioned. It was used to carrying sudden peaks of race traffic for Ascot, Sandown Park, Kempton Park and elsewhere, and crowds of holidaymakers for the Isle of Wight, Bournemouth and many other favourite resorts in Dorset, Devon and Cornwall.

The LSWR also owned an ocean port at Southampton that was challenging Liverpool; no other railway possessed in its own right such an important terminal for deep-sea passenger traffic, despite the Great Western's attempt to build up Plymouth and Fishguard. The South Western's freight was also far from negligible, ranging from Cornish china clay to imports of all kinds through Southampton together with a wide range of domestic agricultural products; coals and manufactured articles flowed to the south and west, via Feltham yard, from the north and Midlands.

Above all, the LSWR had enjoyed eleven years of strong leadership from Sir Herbert Walker, guiding it towards electrification and overseeing the final phases of reconstruction at Waterloo. Walker's authority had now become unchallenged, despite a few early brushes with that formidable locomotive engineer, Dugald Drummond, whose untimely accidental death soon terminated any problem there. Clashes with Henry Holmes, the Superintendent of the Line, who had cherished hopes of the general managership, had been more serious and had been solved only by Holmes's accelerated retirement.

Walker's thinking, particularly on the advantages of standardised departure times or 'clock-face' services, had greatly improved the operating performance and removed some former LSWR oddities, such as starting an express with several stops only minutes before a faster second train with fewer stops. That had been the sort of thing that had led Rudyard Kipling to write in *My Sunday at Home*: 'On Sundays all things are possible on the London and South Western.'

The LSWR's chief contribution to Southern Railway stations was the new Waterloo, which had been under reconstruction for many years since the first steps were taken towards modernising the higgledy-piggledy collection of train sheds that had grown up after 1848. Reconstruction had been a protracted affair – many might think too protracted – but it reached a triumphant conclusion when Queen Mary opened the Victory Arch, the main entrance to the new station, on 21 March 1922. She was deputising for King George V, who had a cold; the notoriously windy entrance at the top of a long flight of steps was known to the staff as 'Pneumonia Corner' and the King's doctors advised him not to stand there on a chilly day.

Rebuilding may be considered to have started in 1878 when the first South Station was built. It was also known to the staff as 'Cyprus', that island having been ceded to Britain in the previous year. The North, or Windsor, Station was opened in sections between 1884 and 1885, looking very much as it does today, and was also given a topical name, 'Khartoum'. The present South Station was opened in 1910.

But the main task, reconstructing the jumble of main line platforms and tracks in the centre of the station, did not start

11

until 1911. Modernisation was carried out by working from south to north. An important amenity was added in 1919, an escalator connection to the Underground and the Waterloo & City tube. The complex of station offices along platform 16 known to the staff as the 'Village' was completed in 1920.

The most important part of this huge task fell upon the shoulders of J. W. Jacomb-Hood, the railway's Chief Engineer from 1901 to 1914, though it was finished off by his successor, A. W. Szlumper. After 1912 there was considerable guidance on all policy aspects from Sir Herbert Walker. Waterloo today, despite some internal remodelling, remains a memorial to these great figures of the LSWR. Pevsner has called Waterloo – at any rate, the offices with the curving facade by J. R. Scott – 'the only 20th century station in London with architectural ambitions'. (He was writing before the reconstruction of Euston.) The Victory Arch, which is the LSWR war memorial, is flanked by statues which not many who pass through it realise are supposed to represent War and Peace. Above the arch rides Britannia. It is a pity, however, that Waterloo's impressiveness can scarcely be appreciated from any of the streets which surround it. It is in fact best seen from the windows of a train leaving Charing Cross, since the South Eastern viaduct runs opposite the main Waterloo façade before entering Waterloo (Eastern), formerly Waterloo Junction. That name arose from the single track that originally traversed the concourse of the LSWR station and then entered the SER station. This rail link had been used for Royal Trains from Windsor to Dover for the Continent, for troop trains and for empty carriage workings, after its earlier use for some very roundabout London suburban services had come to an end. Later the track was lifted and the bridge was converted to a footway; but until its removal in 1985 a section of the former platform on the bridge, complete with awning, remained – an interesting survival.

Other LSWR stations tended to be rather cramped and cheaply built, with the exception of Bournemouth Central (called East until 1899), where an impressive new building was put up in 1888. It had a high glazed roof covering four tracks between two platforms; a local writer had described it as 'designed to look like a Winter Garden in a natural dell'. But

12

Exeter (Queen Street), Woking, Southampton West and other important stations needing modernisation had to await the coming of the Southern Railway.

Stations of real historic interest or architectural merit were not many on the LSWR. One must except Southampton Terminus, designed by Sir William Tite and dating from 1840, and his contemporary Nine Elms terminal, demoted to goods offices when Waterloo was opened in 1848.

But there were some substantial engineering works: a fine succession of flyovers or dive-unders, the first of which had come at Twickenham in 1888, provided unobstructed junction facilities. Leading to or from the main line, they were sited at Raynes Park, Malden, Hampton Court Junction (an impressive combination of a viaduct, flyover and a dive-under), Byfleet, Pirbright, and Worting, beyond Basingstoke. Tunnels, however, were short in contrast with those of the other two constituent railways. Viaducts also were not very noteworthy, apart from Meldon viaduct in Cornwall, one of the few steel viaducts in Britain, as well as the unique viaduct at Cannington on the Lyme Regis branch, constructed in concrete and dating from 1903.

In signalling the South Western was quite advanced in its use of lock-and-block. It had also installed semi-automatic low-pressure pneumatic working of the signals on the busy four-track section from Woking to Basingstoke in 1901. This embodied a feature entirely contrary to usual British railway practice, a normal 'clear' position instead of the normal 'danger'.

In late Victorian and Edwardian times all the south of England's railway companies had stood low in public esteem compared with the major northern lines, largely on account of their relatively poor coaching stock. This reputation was only partly deserved. Certainly, to the south of London the likelihood of travelling in a four- or six-wheeled vehicle persisted long after the wealthier companies had equipped themselves with bogie carriages. But around the turn of the century the LSWR, under the influence of the Carriage and Wagon Engineer W. Panter, who was ex-LNWR and Wolverton-trained, embarked upon considerable modernisation of the carriage stock. This really started with the ornate 'American Eagle' bogie stock of 1890,

13

built for the Plymouth Ocean Liner specials. These carriages had side corridors but were not gangwayed to each other. They lasted a long time; the Southern Railway was later to use them on the South Eastern Division in conjunction with Pullmans.

Closely following came an extensive build of lavatory, non-gangwayed vehicles, widely used over the LSWR. Kipling, in the story mentioned above, referred to 'the first-class lavatory compartment which the London and South Western Railway sometimes supply without extra charge'. Lavatories were essential for the long-distance West of England expresses, and desirable for the Bournemouth and Portsmouth services.

Surrey Warner succeeded Panter in 1906. His background had been the Great Western, and his introduction of the clerestory into LSWR carriage design may have reflected Swindon practice; he built the first dining cars for the LSWR, incorporating that feature, in 1906. He also built the four sleeping-cars used in connection with the services put on to compete with the GWR to and from Plymouth, serving the ocean liner sailings in 1904. After the Salisbury accident of 1906 (the cause of the excessive speed that led to the disastrous derailment was never ascertained) the cars were sold to the GWR.

Warner also built in 1921 four sets of five cars for the Bournemouth line equipped with 'pantries'; the first steam stock to be painted in dark green. For the 1915 electrification, a number of older four- and six-wheeled compartment bodies were mounted on new frames and bogies. They were, moreover, painted green and had been the first to depart from the LSWR's salmon-and-brown. On the whole, therefore, the railway's passenger stock was not too bad by contemporary standards, though it was still far from rivalling the excellence of, say, the Midland Railway. The LSWR was even slower to abolish second-class travel than the LBSCR; it did so in 1918, six years after the 'Brighton', usually considered ultra-conservative, had done so.

If overmuch attention may appear to be paid to coaching stock, it is because the age and condition of the carriages (and unpunctuality) were the main sources of criticism of railways that in many other respects might be considered well managed.

14

These criticisms came to a head after the end of the First World War.

The LSWR's locomotives were a mixed bag, some as impressive in appearance as any to be seen elsewhere, like Dugald Drummond's 'Paddleboxes'; and others remarkably old-fashioned, for example the Adams 0-4-2s still used for secondary main line work, such as services from Waterloo to Gosport via Alton. The LSWR's legacy to the Southern in this respect is described in Chapter 4, including the changes effected by Drummond's successor, Urie, who had been in charge since 1912.

The London Brighton & South Coast

The 'Brighton' was a highly individual railway. Perhaps on this account, its character was to be changed quite markedly once it was absorbed into the Southern. It had no pretensions to being a major trunk line. Its longest services were from London to Portsmouth (87 miles) and Hastings (76 miles), and to both of these places there were faster trains by a competitor with a shorter route. The railway's 'flagship' service was to Brighton, only 51 miles. Speeds were never very high on any of the routes. But its standing with the public rose gradually in the years before the First World War. In Victorian times it had been criticised for high fares, and it was one of the last railways to admit third-class passengers to all its trains. Its weakest spot had been the London suburban services, mostly provided by rather Spartan six-wheeled carriages pulled by small tank engines. The electrification of London's trams in the early part of the twentieth century had hit the Brighton hard, with the South Metropolitan Electric Tramways and the London County Council system abstracting much of the inner suburban traffic, whilst Croydon Corporation's trams competed further south.

The Brighton's answer had been electrification, which it had carried out in three main stages. The South London line came first in 1909, and the Crystal Palace line in 1911, with the last stage before the grouping, to Tulse Hill and West Norwood, in 1912. It had thus moved ahead of the LSWR in this respect.

Moreover, unlike the South Western, its electrification system had been chosen with a deliberate eye to its eventual extension over the main lines, first to Brighton and then probably to Portsmouth. It was the single-phase alternating-current system at 6,600 volts, with overhead current collection.

That system had been recommended for general adoption by Sir Philip Dawson, the eminent consulting electrical engineer; it was rejected by Walker and the LSWR Board on several grounds. But the LBSCR did not regret its decision, though there was criticism of its placing of the contract for electrical equipment with the AEG (Allgemeine Elektrizitäts Gesellschaft) of Germany rather than a British firm. Certainly the travelling public appreciated the comfort and cleanliness of the new trains, smoother-riding than the LSWR electric stock even if the acceleration was rather sluggish. The LBSC advertised the South London line as 'Elevated Electric' as a counterpart perhaps to the 'Underground'; although, unlike the Liverpool Overhead or the New York Elevated, only a part (though a substantial one) of the journey was on viaduct. Not only was the traffic lost to the trams regained, but new traffic had been gained as well.

The Brighton's contribution to the steam locomotive stock inherited by the Southern is discussed in Chapter 4.

So far as passenger carriages are concerned, the number of antiquated non-bogie carriages was still very high by the standards of the more progressive northern railways. William Stroudley had just started the building of bogie stock in 1889, long after the Midland or the LNWR; in that year he put a set (first class only, of course) in the 'City Limited' service, 8.45 am from Brighton to London Bridge, returning at 5 pm. In 1898 A. H. Panter (the son of W. Panter of the LSWR) had been appointed Carriage and Wagon Works Manager and helped the introduction of more modern stock generally. By 1900 some bogie vehicles in block train sets were being built for suburban services. But, apart from the 'City Limited' and the Pullman cars which started to be provided in 1875, non-corridor carriages were still the rule even on the 'fast' trains (as the LBSCR always designated its expresses, sometimes with doubtful justification).

Better vehicles appeared in the shape of the 'Balloon' stock, so-called because of its very high elliptical roofs, and also the electric stock for the South London and the Crystal Palace lines. The South London sets had some semi-corridors, which enabled passengers to distribute themselves through a carriage after boarding it, and thus reduce station stopping times – an important consideration in view of the fact that the South London scheme was expressly intended to win passengers back from the electric trams by offering quicker services.

The Brighton's first all-Pullman train had started in 1881. The steam-hauled 'Southern Belle', much loved by Brighton visitors, started to run in 1908 and lasted until it was replaced by the electric 'Brighton Belle' under Southern Railway auspices in 1935.

One might summarise by describing the LBSCR as a curious mixture of the progressive and the old-fashioned. Progressive it certainly was in station construction, to an extent that put some of the northern lines to shame. The reconstruction of Victoria, completed in 1908, was a most ingenious and effective piece of replanning. Widening was restricted by the SECR station on one side and Buckingham Palace Road on the other, so the station was lengthened – some platforms by as much as 300 yards – and intermediate running roads with crossovers were installed between the platform roads so that some platforms could hold two trains, each able to arrive or depart independently. The handsome frontage of the Grosvenor Hotel, in the French Renaissance manner, was extended to become a new façade for the rebuilt train shed by the LBSCR Chief Engineer, Sir Charles Morgan.

Unhappily, London Bridge was not given the same treatment – even though its range of Italianate buildings, originally designed by David Mocatta but much rebuilt, housed the Company's headquarter offices. It remained something of a muddle even in Southern Railway days.

Elsewhere the Brighton stations were usually good and sometimes charming – for instance at Boxhill, and at Leatherhead, where the architect C. H. Driver allowed himself some French influence. Brighton Central retained the original Mocatta building (somewhat spoilt by awnings over the roadway in front) but the train shed had been completely rebuilt

17

in 1883 by H. E. Wallis, using the technique applied at Waterloo of constructing a new roof over the existing one and then demolishing the older structure.

Eastbourne was a good edifice with its clock tower – a feature often found on the LBSC. Excellent stations with spacious platforms existed at Streatham Common, Thornton Heath, Norbury and Crystal Palace Low Level in the suburban area. Further afield, Lewes had been rebuilt in 1887 and there were good buildings at East Grinstead, Christ's Hospital, Sheffield Park, Horsted Keynes and Hassocks. One curiosity at Forest Hill was the surviving building of the 'Atmospheric Engine House', originally built when the London & Croydon Railway was experimenting with that system in 1845.

A few black spots remained in the suburban area, such as the poverty-stricken wooden shack at Peckham Rye. On the main lines, Chichester and Littlehampton were poor.

The LBSCR could be snobbish: at Singleton on the Chichester-Midhurst single-line branch a most imposing station with four platforms was built for the smart Goodwood race traffic.

So far as running facilities were concerned, the Brighton had been progressive. Since 1910 there were four tracks on the main line from London as far as the north end of Balcombe tunnel, getting rid of the problem of the SECR share in the 'old' pair of tracks, now downgraded to slow lines by the construction of the 'Quarry' lines bypassing Redhill. Elsewhere the provision of flyovers and dive-unders in the London suburban area – especially the complex at Selhurst, more reminiscent of French than British railway practice – enabled parallel movements to be made which greatly assisted the operation of a heavy commuter traffic.

Unlike the South Western, the Brighton had a fine collection of long tunnels. The main line between London and Brighton traversed the North Downs, the Forest Ridge and the South Downs, in each case by means of a notable tunnel. Quarry (North Downs) was 1 mile 353 yards long and Clayton (South Downs) 1 mile 499 yards. There were plenty of tunnels on the subsidiary lines too. Some of the latter, incidentally, were valued as offering diversionary routes to Brighton in the event of the

18

main line being blocked, the most vulnerable spots being the tunnels and the Ouse viaduct. This latter is a splendid and much-photographed structure, the happy product of J. U. Rastrick's engineering and David Mocatta's embellishment. Even more striking from some viewpoints is the great London Road viaduct at Brighton.

The LBSC was also progressive in its signalling. Sykes lock-and-block, offering safeguards not incorporated in the ordinary block telegraph system, covered the working of the busy London suburban area, as well as much of the main line. On most railways the distant signal at night showed merely a red light which drivers were expected to identify from the location as meaning 'caution' instead of 'stop'. The Brighton helped its drivers by providing an illuminated white fishtail sign beside the red lamp to distinguish it, the so-called 'Coligny-Welch' lamp.

The Brighton operated a continental service between Newhaven and Dieppe, in conjunction with the État Company in France, which was the shortest in crow's-flight mileage between London and Paris. It could not be the quickest because of the sea distance (64 nautical miles against 21 between Dover and Calais) but it could be and was the cheapest. The ships were always well-found, but the LBSC 'continental' stock (non-corridor 'Balloons' as a rule), together with the rather Spartan amenities at Newhaven, suggested that travellers would be drawn to it for reasons of economy rather than prestige.

All in all, the Brighton was a highly individual line in its strengths and weaknesses; it was to experience drastic changes under Southern management which older members of the staff would not always accept gracefully – certainly not its last General Manager, who despite his Chatham origin had become the most dyed-in-the-wool Brightonian of them all. For many years Victoria displayed a splendid wall map of the LBSCR in glazed tiles, showing its pride in the system.

The South Eastern & Chatham

Before the First World War broke out in 1914, the South Eastern & Chatham Railways Managing Committee had had a decade and a half in which to redeem its two component

19

systems, the South Eastern and the London Chatham & Dover, from the shortcomings that each had shown and which had been aggravated by thirty years of mutual antagonism. A lot of progress had been made; rationalisation of routes outside London had taken place, much facilitated by the linking of the two main lines by the system of spurs known variously as the Chislehurst Curves or the Bickley Junctions. Both railways had been much criticised for the poor quality of their rolling stock, mostly four- or six-wheeled, while the northern lines had long been building bogie vehicles. Lavatories were still provided rather grudgingly and usually for first- and second-class passengers only. Gangwayed stock was almost unknown until 1921.

However, the SER had built a few bogie suburban sets as early as the 1880s, and both the component systems of the SECR had experimented with luxury train sets of foreign design. The SER introduced an 'American Car Train' on its Hastings line in 1892, and some vehicles of this design were afterwards run on the Folkestone service in 1897. The LCDR had a 'Club Train' in 1889–93, running to the Kent coast resorts; however, this was not based on American carriage design but comprised vehicles supplied by the European Wagons-Lits Company. Neither service lasted long.

An SECR curiosity was the Continental Royal Saloon kept at Calais for the continental journeys of the Prince of Wales (later Edward VII), owned originally by the SER. It was 58 feet long and ran on six-wheeled bogies. It had been ordered by Sir Edward Watkin when Chairman of that Company from the carriage works of his other major railway, the Manchester Sheffield & Lincolnshire, whose engineer (T. Parker) and staff were employed on the job. The saloon lasted until 1929 on the Southern Railway.

In 1921, however, the SECR introduced a quantity of gangwayed, side-corridor vehicles for the continental services which were very up-to-date. They had straight sides and panelling which gave them an un-English look. Oddly, the end vehicles (semi-brake) in each set had no gangway connections at their outside ends. A few corridor vehicles had previously been built by Wainwright, largely for through working to other railways.

The Southern's coat of arms

Opening of the Victory Arch at Waterloo, March 1922

3   The Waterloo Station of the London
Necropolis Company

4   Necropolis terminus in the cemetery at
Brookwood

5 'Southern Belle' hauled by a '13' 4-4-2T, no. 90

6 A Reading train near Betchworth in August 1932

7 The Hythe–Sandgate horse tramway

8   Sir Herbert Walker

9   Brig.-General The Hon. Everard Baring

10   Robert Holland–Martin

11   Sir Eustace Missenden

12   A 'T14' on a Portsmouth express passing Surbiton in 1926

13   Maunsell's rebuild of L. B. Billinton's 4-6-4T as a tender engine (Class 'N15X')

14   No. 801 'Sir Meliot de Logres' of the 'King Arthur' class at Victoria

15   Maunsell's masterpiece: 'Schools' class no. 900 'Eton' on a Charing Cross–Deal train,
about 1931

16 Power-car of the original LSWR Waterloo and City 'tube'

17 Power house of the LSWR at Durnsford Road, Wimbledon

18 'Overhead electric' train entering Crystal Palace High Level station

19 Problems of the third rail in winter!

The locomotive stock was on the whole pretty good. Before R. E. L. Maunsell came from Inchicore to Ashford, both systems had been equipped by W. Kirtley and H. S. Wainwright with locomotives of essentially conventional design – practically all inside-cylinder engines, mainly of the classic 4–4–0, 0–6–0 and 0–4–4T wheel arrangements, which performed well and reliably, though naturally some classes outshone others. Maunsell had big ideas, including a 4–6–0 express passenger design for the SECR which civil engineering restrictions forced him to shelve until Southern Railway days.

The South Eastern was noted for its neat and tidy track yet, oddly enough, it imposed a universal maximum line speed of 60 mph, usually observed by drivers except for occasional bouts of exuberance. The 'Chatham' had no such restriction and its switchback main line, especially between Swanley and the top of the Sole Street bank leading down to the Medway crossing, lent itself to bursts of quite high speed. The boneshaking experienced by passengers in bumpy four- or six-wheeled, short-wheelbase carriages must sometimes have been acute.

But the SECR was often surprisingly forward-looking. It recruited more people with higher educational backgrounds than the LSWR, where starting at the bottom and relying solely on practical experience was pretty well universal. The SECR had some affinity here with the London & North Western, which was often described as a very 'gentlemanly' railway. It was relevant that Sir Francis Dent, SECR General Manager from 1911 to 1920 (and previously Goods Manager), had come from the LNWR. And Maunsell, Irish by birth, had had Crewe training before he went to the Great Southern & Western Railway of Ireland, where Inchicore works had quite a tradition of Crewe-trained chiefs and Crewe workshop practices.

The SECR's plans for the future included the long-overdue electrification of its complex suburban network. Characteristically, perhaps, it disdained to follow the lead of either the LSWR (third rail DC at 600V) or the LBSCR with its overhead AC system at 6,600V. It favoured instead a high-voltage DC system with a protected live rail, but its planning had not taken shape as a project by the time war broke out in 1914 and so it was shelved 'for the duration'.

The SECR had quite a substantial freight traffic, much of which it carried in open wagons of a very distinctive design, with high rounded ends which assisted, by means of a stretcher bar, the sheeting of loads when required. There was continental traffic (some handled at the 'Grande Vitesse' depot at Blackfriars), much coal including that from the Kent field, together with industrial materials received from the northern lines, agricultural produce and livestock.

A special feature was the 'hoppers' specials' which catered for the mass movement of Cockneys into the hop fields in early autumn for a few weeks of camping out and hard work picking the hops, with a certain holiday atmosphere. For these trains, usually starting from New Cross for the south Londoners, the SECR dug out its most ancient four- and six-wheelers to rattle along to wayside stations in the Kentish Weald, especially Paddock Wood.

The SECR was certainly not renowned for fine stations. Charing Cross and Cannon Street were simple train sheds tucked behind substantial hotel buildings. Of its country stations, those on the Hastings line had most appeal – especially Battle, built in 1853 by the architect W. Tress, and Etchingham. However, it did get round to building an impressive structure at Dover Marine, finished just in time for the 1914–18 wartime traffic, replacing the old station on the Admiralty Pier.

As regards engineering works, the most significant were those on the joint line with the LBSCR (the 'old' main line) between Coulsdon (Stoat's Nest, as it was then called) and Redhill; on the New Cross to Tonbridge cut-off opened in 1868; and between Folkestone and Dover. The first-named stretch included the (old) Merstham tunnel (1 mile 71 yards) and some deep cuttings. The cut-off route, or new main line via Sevenoaks, saving 13 miles compared with the old route via Redhill, included the two longest tunnels that were to come into the Southern Railway, Sevenoaks (1 mile 1,693 yards) and Polhill (1 mile 851 yards), as well as some deep cuttings in the North Downs.

On the last part of the SER's route to Dover there are shorter tunnels at Sandling and Saltwood, the huge Foord viaduct at Folkestone, and the three tunnels in the chalk cliffs between

22

Folkestone and Dover – Abbotscliff, Shakespeare and Martello. This seafront stretch of line, through an area known as the Warren, is prone to serious slippages of chalk. The worst of these occurred in December 1915 and resulted in the closure of the South Eastern route to Dover; it was not reopened until after the end of the war. (A previous slip also closing the line had occurred in 1877.)

It is often remarked that the No. 1 boat-train route from Victoria to Dover, which traverses in addition to Polhill and Sevenoaks, the old Chatham line's Penge tunnel (1 mile 381 yards), is in tunnel for almost 10 per cent of its length.

The SECR had of course suffered in the loss of its continental services during the war, although Service traffic had largely taken over. Dover Marine was invaluable for loading ambulance trains from the ships bringing the wounded from France. The SECR ships had been commandeered by the Admiralty and no less than four had been lost by enemy action. But by the time of the Grouping there had been a good recovery in this profitable business and the main handicap remaining was the weakness of SECR track; much more powerful and heavier locomotives were needed to haul the boat trains, but for the time being nothing bigger than Wainwright 4–4–0s could be used, frequently of course in double-heading. This was a problem almost as serious as that of the suburban traffic, where complaints of slowness, elderly rolling stock and unpunctuality of the steam trains were rife. They provided the new Southern Railway with major headaches.

Chapter 3

WALKER TAKES CONTROL: MEN OF THE SOUTHERN

Authors of railway company histories sometimes give their readers the impression that the General Manager was the final authority on policy matters to the virtual exclusion of the Board, except where a Chairman – such as Sir Edward Watkin or James Staats Forbes – was also the chief executive. In fact, good teamwork between a Chairman and his General Manager, each respecting the other's role, has usually been the recipe for success.

That was certainly the situation on the Southern and Walker was fortunate in all the four Chairmen whom he served. There was none of the friction that existed on, for instance, the Great Western between Viscount Churchill and Sir Felix Pole.

Initially, Walker had an advantage inasmuch as his former Chairman on the LSWR moved over to head the Board of the Southern and the previous excellent relationship between the two men continued. Brigadier-General Sir Hugh Drummond, however, was not the man to trample over the other constituents of the Southern and he had in any case two Deputy Chairmen to look after those interests. Gerald Loder was an LBSCR nominee on the new Board, and the other Deputy, Brigadier-General the Hon. Everard Baring, was a nominee of the SER.

Walker's position was to be quite fortuitously strengthened later by the fact that none of the four Chairmen with whom he worked was in office very long. General Drummond died only a year and seven months after the Southern came into existence; General Baring, who succeeded him, had a rather longer spell with Walker. Even so, Baring died in May 1932 and his successor, Gerald Loder (who became Lord Wakehurst in June 1934), resigned in December 1934, being succeeded by Robert Holland Martin. Although Holland Martin remained Chairman until his death in January 1944, Walker himself retired on 14 October 1937; thus his periods with his four chairmen were:

Drummond	1 year 7 months
Baring	7 years 9 months
Loder	2 years 6 months
Holland Martin	2 years 9 months

The backgrounds of the Chairmen and Walker were dissimilar. Walker was essentially middle-class in origin and upbringing. The son of a doctor, he had intended to follow his father in that profession but shortage of family money obliged him to look for a clerical post, which happened to bring him to the railway, originally the LNWR, where his qualities of integrity, hard work, and a fantastic memory brought him to the notice of many influential figures. But his Chairmen, in accordance with custom, were very much 'upper-crust' social figures – typically, bankers, soldiers (two being generals) and country landowners. Only Gerald Loder varied the pattern by lacking Army connections and having spent some time in politics.

Curiously, *The Times* obituaries of these four Chairmen, in referring to their work for the Southern Railway, often give the impression that the Chairmen decided everything there; Walker's name is not even mentioned in any of them. Conversely, Klapper's book, *Sir Herbert Walker's Southern Railway*, attributes practically everything to Walker, the Chairmen being rather shadowy figures. The balance needs to be rectified.

Brigadier-General Sir Hugh Drummond, Bart, MVO, was a banker and company director as well as having been a soldier (in the militia since 1878) with a very distinguished 1914–18 war record. He was a Devonshire landowner who had first come into contact with the LSWR over the opening of the branch to Budleigh Salterton; this led to his becoming a director of the railway in 1900, Deputy Chairman in 1904 and Chairman in 1911, in which capacity he had recruited Walker from the London & North Western. His relationship with Walker was thus as close as could be. One of his initiatives had been to press Walker to accelerate the rebuilding of Waterloo Station during the war in order to improve the arrangements there for troop movements.

It was naturally, therefore, to Drummond that Walker turned to explain that the weak-kneed Board decision to appoint three General Managers with equal status and duties was not working and that his position was impossible. Drummond and the Board had in fact leant over backwards to avoid giving the impression that the LSWR element intended to dominate the Southern; perhaps it would have been better to grasp this nettle at the outset.

Walker's opposite numbers (all three, incidentally were paid the same salary, £7,500 p.a.) were, first, Sir William Forbes, former General Manager of the LBSCR, who had an Irish background and was the nephew of James Staats Forbes of the LCDR – two ingredients for an independent outlook! Educated partly on the Continent, Forbes had been put on the LCDR by his all-powerful uncle and had risen to be Continental Manager and then Traffic Manager of the Chatham. He was later Assistant General Manager of the SECR and had been General Manager of the Brighton for twenty-four years. His views had now turned into prejudices and he had no use for other than Brighton practices. In this he could count to some extent on the backing of Gerald Loder.

Walker's second coadjutor, Percy Tempest, was an engineer. He was, at sixty-four, three years younger and quite a bit less pugnacious than Forbes. He had become General Manager of the SECR only three years earlier, in succession to a very dominating personality, Sir Francis Dent, who had resigned because of a disagreement with his Chairman, Cosmo Bonsor. Tempest was more co-operative than Forbes, but even so relations were very difficult. Walker continued to work in his office at Waterloo, whilst Forbes remained at London Bridge (LBSCR side) and Tempest at the same station but in the ex-SECR offices.

Walker retained his practice, which he had started at Euston, of chairing a monthly Traffic Officers' Conference on the ex-LSWR side at which the Operating and Commercial Department were fully represented. These meetings dealt with a great range of subjects backed by substantial tables of figures. Train mileage, engine mileage, timetable alterations, incidents of any kind from accidents to minor breaches of the rule book, were all reported and discussed. Traffic receipts, claims and staff matters, including the admission of individuals to super-annuation, were on the agenda, as were all new works, even those costing as little as £30. The receipts at station lavatories were noted and compared with the wages cost of lavatory attendants. It might seem unnecessary to bring to the attention of the General Manager and a team of departmental chiefs the theft from the station till at Worplesdon of the sum of 7/11½d (40p), yet this was done and formally minuted: 'it is recommended that the amount of 7/11½d be cleared' (minute 3671 of January 1923). The suspension for one day of an engine-man who slightly overran a stop signal and a reprimand to a porter were also reported in the minutes. But Walker, with his prodigious memory and appetite for detail, saw nothing incongruous in this nor did it distract him from more weighty policy considerations.

The Board had given the 'triumvirs' a remit to prepare an organisation for the Southern Railway as a whole, but no progress could be made so long as they remained virtually independent of each other. Walker saw Drummond and offered to resign if that would ease the position; Drummond would not hear of this and at last grasped the nettle. He talked to the Board, and it was arranged that Forbes, who was sixty-seven, would retire on 30 June 1923 with a golden hand-shake.

Tempest also was persuaded to retire, on 31 December; he was mellowed by receiving a knighthood in the Birthday Honours, together with an appointment for one year after the end of 1923 as a consultant to the Southern. He even attended Walker's Traffic Conference once, in October 1923; and he came as a guest to the annual dinner of the General Manager's office, held at the Cannon Street Hotel on 24 October 1924, when Walker from the chair paid a tribute to the help that

27

Tempest had given him in the previous difficult period. Tempest died only one month later, on 24 November 1924.

From the middle of 1923, therefore, with Forbes out of the way, Walker could start to pick his own team and at last submit to the Board an organisation for a united railway, to take effect in 1924.

Before dealing with the management it is appropriate to mention that Walker's chief sponsor on the new Board, General Drummond, died sadly early, on 1 August 1924; he was only sixty-four years old. His successor was another general, the Hon. Everard Baring of the famous merchant banking family. He had been Military Secretary to the Viceroy of India and was now a director of several banks and insurance companies; his interest in railways had started in 1913 with the Rhodesia & Mashonaland Railways, where he was involved in reorganisation.

On the Southern he was well able to deal with questions of external relations and public policy, especially over the negotiations about the proposed removal of Charing Cross Station to make way for a road bridge. He was described after his death as 'one of the kindest and bravest of men', and a friend wrote that 'no eyes could express so much amusement'; the nickname of 'The Imp' given him in boyhood stayed with him, so far as intimate friends were concerned, to the end. This would make him an excellent foil to the quiet and serious Walker.

He was barely sixty when he became Chairman and his seven and three-quarter years at Waterloo covered the period of the Southern's major progress, especially electrification. His death on 7 May 1932 must have saddened Walker a great deal. The next Chairman was Gerald Walter Erskine Loder, the fourth son of Sir Robert Loder, who had qualified as a barrister and represented Brighton in Parliament between 1899 and 1905. He had become a Junior Lord of the Treasury in 1905, but his interests were less in politics than in railways and gardening. He had joined the LBSCR Board in 1896 and became Chairman just before Grouping owing to the illness of Charles C. Macrae. His manner was quiet, almost gloomy. But after he died his *Times* obituarist wrote that 'he shared with William Whitelaw of the LNER the reputation of having a more intimate and practical knowledge of railway management and operation than most other railway chairmen or directors . . . like Mr. Whitelaw, he practically confined his business activities to the railway'.

The closeness of his interest may perhaps not have appealed very strongly to Walker, who had had a clear understanding with General Baring of the dividing line between direction and management. Speaking to a meeting of the Retired Railway Officers Society, Loder had expressed regret that in the 1930s Directors were no longer so closely in touch with railway officers, other than the most senior ones, as had been the case before Grouping. Old Brighton loyalties died hard, it seemed.

Gerald Loder's other great love was his superb garden at Wakehurst Place, not far from the Brighton main line, which led to his Presidency of the Royal Horticultural Society and to the most beautiful of all rhododendrons being named *Loderi*.

He received a peerage, as Lord Wakehurst, in 1934 and resigned his chairmanship of the Southern at the end of that year owing to ill health. He was succeeded by Robert Holland Martin, who like Baring came from a famous private banking family and, typically, combined this with a great love of the countryside and also of the Army through the Territorials. Holland Martin was made the subject, after his death, of a 'symposium' volume of studies by family and friends that revealed him as a very attractive character. One essay stressed the appeal that railway work had for him, partly because of its contrast with the world of banking. He would seem to have been content to leave Walker and Frank Dudley Docker to argue the financial implications of a project, and to have been fascinated by the human side of the business which he constantly referred to as 'the Southern family'. Electrification caused him to press strongly for effective protection of the live rail, particularly for the benefit of children and animals. He was also deeply interested in making trains cheerful and attractive: he was personally involved in the decorative treatment of the 'Bognor buffet' cars, and he supported the use of 'malachite green' introduced by Bulleid.

Holland Martin's personality caused much friendly gossip at Waterloo – his habits of losing papers, of having pockets full of what he called 'gadgets' that intrigued him, and also his

29

fondness for driving an ancient open two-seater car, which he did *very* badly, much too fast, along country roads. He was full of varied interests, including archaeology, and enjoyed dressing eccentrically – by no means an orthodox Company Chairman. But his very difference from Walker may well have led to a harmonious relationship, each respecting the other's individual qualities.

Fortunate as Walker may have been in his Chairmen, he had of course to rely on the full Board for formal authority for his proposals. By and large, what the Chairman agreed beforehand with the General Manager usually went through, and the Southern tradition was that Board decisions must be unanimous. To achieve this, there was a tussle over the Eastbourne and Hastings electrification, when doubts about the financial justification had to be overcome; and the scheme for electrifying the South Eastern route to Hastings was actually thrown out in 1937, much to Walker's disappointment. In general, although the Chairmen were all greatly respected City figures, they were not industrialists or accustomed to a detailed analysis of engineering projects. Here Dudley Docker, the West Midlands financier and industrialist, was a key figure and generally helpful to Walker. He appreciated Walker's grasp of finance and also his caution about committing the Company to substantial capital expenditure.

The number of ex-railway General Managers on the Board was also rather remarkable – Sir Charles Owens (Walker's predecessor on the LSWR), Sir Robert Turnbull from the LNWR and Sir Francis Dent of the SECR, not to mention Sir Charles Morgan, ex-Chief Engineer of the LBSCR. Sir Robert Turnbull, who had sponsored Walker years ago on the LNWR, died quite soon, in 1925, but Sir Francis Dent, who had in his time been an autocratic and sometimes difficult character, survived until 1955, when he died at the age of eighty-eight, actually outliving Walker. Dudley Docker lived until 1944 and saw Walker through until both retired in 1937.

By the end of 1923 Walker was able to submit an organisation for a unified Southern Railway to the Board, replacing what had previously been really three railways sharing little except a name and a Board of Directors. He was especially careful to select on the basis of ability irrespective of former Company background; he was determined to avoid the mistake made on the LMS, where people from first one and then, after a few years, another of the constituent railways found themselves on the 'gravy train', whilst others were cold-shouldered.

On the whole, Walker found that the ex-SECR management had much to contribute. From it he drew E. C. Cox as Chief Operating Superintendent and R. E. L. Maunsell as Chief Mechanical Engineer. The Locomotive Running Superintendent, A. D. Jones, was also an ex-SECR man whose responsibilities were threefold: to the General Manager for the administration of his department; to the Chief Operating Superintendent for the provision of locomotive power; and to the Chief Mechanical Engineer for the running maintenance of the locomotives. Another South Eastern man, who was later not merely to occupy Walker's chair at Waterloo but to become the Chairman of British Railways, was E. J. Missenden, who came to London Bridge as Divisional Operating Superintendent, London (East).

From the South Western came several stalwarts upon whom Walker could depend; A. W. Szlumper as Chief Engineer (George Ellson from the SECR was his deputy) and Herbert Jones as Electrical Engineer, bringing with him LSWR experience of electrification. The Brighton seemed to lose out, though not through bias on Walker's part; but it did contribute two chief officers in H. A. Sire as Chief Commercial Manager and Charles A. de Pury as Chief Accountant.

Board appointments which fell outside the General Manager's purview were the Secretary, Godfrey Knight, who took over in May 1923, and William Bishop, the Solicitor – both long-standing colleagues and friends of Walker. No General Manager can afford to have bad relations with a Company Secretary who has the ear of the Chairman and controls the arrangements for Board meetings. Walker was extremely well placed in this respect. William Bishop, in fact, like Walker, had come from the LNWR and it was he who had suggested to Drummond that Walker would be the best man to succeed Sir Charles Owens in 1912.

It is fortunate for historians that Sir John Elliot, who came to

Waterloo in 1925 as Mr J. B. Elliot to work directly under Walker, has given a superb word-picture of Walker, both of the man and his managerial style. Elliot's autobiography and his long article in the *Journal of Transport History* of November 1960 entitled 'Early Days of the Southern Railway' must be quoted if a later generation is to envisage Walker correctly. There are very few such accounts by an insider of just how a great railway was managed, especially when written by an insider who is also an author. Elliot describes Walker:

> He was a big man physically – grey-haired, deliberate in his walk, firm of feature, quiet of voice. His seniority and his outstanding ability ensured his place as undisputed 'Chief', yet there was nothing at all of the dictator in him, and that was part of his strength. You could put your case before him, and he would listen. A few questions, always to the heart of the matter, and then he would give you a decision. And he would stick to it.
>
> With the Board he was always careful not to usurp, or even seem to usurp, their function of direction and ultimate sanction, but he was equally – and immovably – determined that management was his and his alone, to be delegated, of course, to his Chief Officers as he thought fit. There were a few occasions when an over-zealous or self-important director stepped across the line, but it seldom happened twice. Walker would seek him out, point out his unwisdom, and if necessary invoke the Chairman. It never failed.

Walker was not perfect, of course. Unlike Frank Pick of London Transport, he had no real interest in the environmental aspects of the railway; nor had he great social talents. Klapper comments in his biography: 'If Walker had a fault, it was the lack of small talk, the shy restraint that held him from conviviality.' But he sought to overcome this failing by assiduously memorising in advance the names of all grades of railway staff whom he might expect to meet on an inspection, so as to help them talk frankly with him about their work.

The secret of Walker's success seems to have been his ability to pick an effective team, to inspire their complete loyalty and thereby to achieve his own policies without bullying – merely by quiet authority. The key to his organisation was, in military terms, a good chief of staff and this he found in Edwin Cox. Cox was a hard worker and a hard taskmaster; he was a far more extrovert character than Walker but he was also a very religious man and there was much of the lay preacher in him, for he was fond of making long speeches. His integrity was complete and he was the ideal executant of Walker's policies. As Chief Operating Superintendent he had as deputy Frank Bushrod, a fine ex-LSWR character with a huge Edwardian moustache, who had worked his way up from the ranks in true roughshod LSWR fashion and now accepted working under a 'South Eastern' man to his surprise.

R. E. L. Maunsell, from Ireland, could sometimes show a touch of temperament – Elliot describes him as able and irascible, a bit of a Tartar. · He was, however, a good administrator as well as a successful locomotive designer; his staff loyally supported him.

A. W. Szlumper, Chief Engineer, was 'bluff, chunky and capable'. He had an equally bluff son, Gilbert, who had been Walker's personal assistant before the war and the valued Secretary of the Railway Executive Committee during the war and now became Docks and Marine Manager. Outspoken, energetic and likeable, Gilbert had a close and happy relationship with Walker – rather surprising, it might seem, in view of his fondness for telling naughty stories, which no one could ever imagine Walker relishing.

Herbert Jones, who had carried through the pioneer electrification schemes on the LSWR, now had to accept that A. W. Raworth, tough, opinionated and effective, was in charge of the Southern's new schemes. Raworth, not very popular with his colleagues, was trusted by Walker for his sheer ability, and in return he loyally supported his General Manager, if few other people. Raworth's independent status was emphasised by his receiving in July 1925 the title of Electrical Engineer (New Works).

Walker's views on organisation, as reflected in the proposals he put to the Board and which came into effect on 1 January 1924, were in line with contemporary thinking. He favoured a departmental structure for the Southern, no doubt intended to prevent old loyalties from hindering the emergence of the Southern as a unified railway. A strongly decentralised organisation such as that of the LNER, a much larger and more geographically dispersed system than the Southern, would have delayed getting away from the confusion prevailing in 1923 of three 'Southern' railways, separately managed. So, although the terms Western, Central and Eastern Sections were in common use, they were geographical rather than managerial concepts. Divisional boundaries for operating purposes did not necessarily conform to former company networks.

Walker also initially favoured separate Operating and Commercial departments – though by 1930 he had changed his views. The logic of such a split, originally introduced by Sir George Gibb on the North Eastern Railway, was that there should be a customer-and-supplier relationship between these two great departments. That was impossible in the traditional Superintendent of the Line organisation, where a single officer was in charge of operation and all aspects of passenger commercial work. E. C. Cox and H. A. Sire were thus nominally equal in status, though Cox's ideas were always closest to Walker's.

Below Operating Headquarters came, initially, six Divisions. London (East), working from London Bridge Station, took most of the ex-SECR and ex-LBSCR suburban areas. Eastern, based on Ashford at first and later on Dover, virtually took the SECR outside the suburban area. London (West), based on Waterloo, covered the ex-LSWR suburban area and the main lines to Southampton and Portsmouth. Southern (based on Brighton) covered the ex-LBSCR beyond the suburban area, together with the Hastings line from Tunbridge Wells. Central, based on Southampton, covered the Basingstoke–Salisbury part of the main line, plus Southampton–Dorchester and branches. Western, based on Exeter, covered the ex-LSWR west of Salisbury. Seven engineering districts, with boundaries not precisely coterminous with the Divisions, were also created.

By 1930 Walker had revised his views. The separation between Operating and Commercial work, logical in theory, was not really valuable on the Southern, where 75 per cent of the traffic receipts came from passengers and where Cox's timetable planning (in which Walker took a keen personal interest) was itself a major commercial activity. A Traffic Department embracing all operating and commercial functions was therefore approved by the Board in February 1930, coming into effect when H. A. Sire retired as Commercial Manager. Cox became Traffic Manager with below him a Superintendent of Operation (Frank Bushrod) and a Commercial Assistant (G. H. Wheeler). Cox had in addition the Continental business, covered by F. A. Brant (Assistant for Continental Traffic). He was also aided by H. E. O. (Toby) Wheeler as General Assistant, and by L. W. Judd as Indoor Assistant. A great deal of interdepartmental co-ordination work was thereby lifted from the shoulders of the General Manager and placed on those of the Traffic Manager.

Several other organisational changes were instituted during this period. A London (Central) Division was created, which embraced most of the ex-LBSCR system, apart from London Bridge, which continued under the control of London (East). Per contra, London (Central) took over the former SECR side of Victoria as well as the Brighton side. The former SER route from Redhill to Reading was divided at Guildford, the eastern portion becoming London (Central) and the western one London (West). Also about this time, a District Freight Superintendent was established to control the London goods depots and Thames wharves, etc., and a South Coast Commercial Representative (located at Brighton) to appease any local feeling about the loss of a Divisional Superintendent at Brighton.

A minor change was the renaming of Central Division, sited at Southampton, as Southern, to avoid any confusion with London (Central).

A very significant move was that of J. B. Elliot away from the General Manager's office, to become Assistant to Traffic Manager for Development of Traffic. Elliot's work in 'selling' the Southern as Public Relations Assistant to the General Manager (described in Chapter 6) since 1925 had been of great commercial importance and he had been doing in effect much of what Sire's department could have been expected to do. His move into the Traffic Department was intended to bring him into the mainstream of railway work, giving him the experience that would later be a qualification for senior managerial office.

Two appointments of future high-fliers were those of E. J. Missenden as Assistant Superintendent of Operation and of R. M. T. (Dickie) Richards as London (West) Divisional Superintendent.

Reorganisations of this kind are not achieved without some degree of blood-letting. Walker took the opportunity of weeding out some officers; no less than eight, with ages ranging from fifty-three to sixty-four, were prematurely retired. It was scarcely a 'night of the long knives', but it showed how tough Walker could be if he felt it necessary. There was no question of finding sinecures for those displaced by the new organisation.

The Traffic organisation remained in force long after Walker's retirement. But a new generation of chief officers began to arrive after 1937; individuals will be discussed in the chapters dealing with the post-Walker period.

Chapter 4

LOCOMOTIVE AND ROLLING STOCK POLICY UNDER MAUNSELL

At the Grouping, the new Southern Railway inherited a fleet of 2,281 steam locomotives, in 108 classes. They came from the three main constituents and several minor railways such as those in the Isle of Wight, and the Plymouth Devonport & South Western Junction. This, of course, was small when compared with the London Midland & Scottish total of over 10,200, but it was still quite a sizeable fleet and the large number of classes demonstrated that it contained no major element of standardisation. There was no general-purpose workhorse built in very large numbers, such as Derby, Crewe and Swindon had bequeathed to the LMS and the Great Western. The survivors of Stroudley's standardisation policy on the LBSCR from 1870 to 1889 were getting thin on the ground. The largest classes of really useful, reliable machines were probably, from the LSWR, the Adams 0–4–2 tender engines and 0–4–4T tank engines, Drummond's 4–4–0 T9 class (a splendid passenger engine) and his M7 0–4–4T series for local train services. From the LBSC came no less than 108 of Stroudley's D1 and D1X 0–4–2T class; and from the SECR 108 of Wainwright's C class 0–6–0 goods engines. Most of these work-horses were pretty elderly by 1923.

The Southern's inheritance of antiques included South Eastern Railway R class 0–6–0T engines built by James Stirling in 1888–98 and used on the steep Folkestone Harbour branch in pairs or threes, even fours at times. There were also tank engines from the London Chatham & Dover Railway dating from 1884 and some even older 0–6–0 goods engines from the same railway, all built by William Kirtley, the oldest in the latter class (B1) dating from 1877. Beattie well-tank 2–4–0T engines originally built from 1874 to 1875 were still at work on the oldest section of the LSWR, the Bodmin and Wadebridge, and the Wenford Bridge branch; some of these were to survive well into the nationalisation era. The very oldest was probably the Isle of Wight Railway's 2–4–0T 'Ryde', built in 1864.

The showpieces, the express passenger types, included Drummond's huge, impressive 4–6–0s in several classes including the famous 'Paddleboxes'; none, however, despite their power, were quite as free-steaming or free-running as his smaller 4–4–0 designs, including the D15s, the 'Bulldogs' and of course the 'Greyhound' T9s. The LBSCR was represented by the Marsh Atlantics, so closely resembling their Great Northern ancestor, and also by the huge L. B. Billinton-designed 4–6–4Ts in class L, of which there were seven. There were also two 4–6–2T express engines (J class) and 27 4–4–2T express engines in class I3. The SECR contributed some excellent express passenger engines, all 4–4–0s (to which wheel arrangement they were restricted by weak bridges on the main line) in Wainwright's D, E and L classes, some rebuilt by Maunsell.

Who was going to take charge of this rather mixed bag of engines, with many classes containing but a few examples, and with the prospect of overall contraction because of the declared intention to electrify suburban services – even though how, and when, was still unsettled? Robert Urie, who had succeeded the formidable Dugald Drummond on the LSWR in 1912, was a less autocratic personality than his predecessor; he had been Works Manager at Eastleigh and was a sound all-round locomotive engineer. He had built some strong, reliable locomotives, unconventional in appearance with their high running plates, easy to maintain, for both fast passenger and heavy goods work. Born in 1854, however, he was now due for retirement.

Lawson Billinton from the LBSCR might have been entitled to hope for the new position, being younger than Urie and even than Maunsell of the SECR. He was a thorough 'Brighton' man, his father, R. J. Billinton, having been Locomotive Superintendent of that railway from 1890 to 1905. But he had been away during the war and was overshadowed by Maunsell, Chief Mechanical Engineer (a grander title than Locomotive Superintendent) of the SECR since 1913. Maunsell had come from a similar post on the Great Southern & Western Railway of Ireland, and he had chaired the Railway Executive Committee's Locomotive Committee during the war. As an engineer, he had been much influenced by the ideas that Swindon had been developing in the field of long-travel valves and the smoothing of steam passages to assist free running. He had built up a strong team on the SECR at Ashford works, and his reputation as a highly progressive engineer, in touch with ideas elsewhere, thus led to his selection by Walker and the Board in preference to Urie or Billinton. He was to remain in office throughout the period of Walker's leadership. He was a man of total integrity – and he never built a poor engine, despite a few problems.

Locomotive history shows quite a number of cases in which a basically sound design has been improved to a startling extent by an engineer content to accept the broad concept of his predecessor in office, and merely to improve it in detail. The new touch might be superheating, or raised boiler pressure, or longer-travel valves, or modified exhaust passages – the result usually a major improvement in performance, changing the adequate into the successful.

Maunsell had the good sense, or the insight, to achieve just this. He continued to develop Wainwright's 4–4–0s into the splendid L class for the ex-SECR main line. Similarly, he built on foundations laid by Drummond and Urie; the latter's H15 class of 4–6–0 became, when modified, the first batch of King Arthurs built in Southern Railway days, the combined fleet taking over express passenger work with great success.

For some time after Grouping a unified locomotive policy seemed slow to appear: both LSWR and SECR designs were perpetuated, with some modifications, by the new Chief Mechanical Engineer; only Brighton dropped out. Until 1931 the locomotives continued to carry their old pre-Grouping numbers. The ex-LSWR engines had the prefix 'E', for Eastleigh; ex-LBSCR ones 'B' for Brighton; and ex-SECR ones 'A' for Ashford; whilst the little collection of 18 from the Isle of Wight railways were indicated by 'W'. Soon, however, all

Southern locomotives began to have their numbers painted very large on the tender, a practice that Maunsell had started on the SECR.

In effect, development of pre-Grouping policies continued until about 1926. On the South Eastern side, Maunsell continued to build the two classes which he had been able to originate during the First World War, namely the 2–6–0 class N mixed traffic locomotive, and the 2–6–4T of class K. The first of these types was a very modern-looking machine with outside Walschaerts valve gear, 200 lb psi steam pressure and a taper boiler. Steam collection was by means of a perforated pipe above the top corner of the firebox, the dome being used to accommodate the boiler top-feed apparatus, and there also were long-travel valves – all features reflecting Swindon principles. It was highly successful and adopted by the government as a standard type for locomotive building at Woolwich Arsenal in order to alleviate unemployment caused by the cessation of munitions production.

The Southern Railway inherited 16 of these fine engines from the SECR, and further building was commissioned at Ashford in 1923 with another batch being built from components manufactured at Woolwich. As late as 1933 a further series was put in hand at Ashford, so that the Southern eventually had a substantial number of these useful machines. They were mainly in two-cylinder form (N and U classes) with a small number of three-cylinder examples (N1 and U1). The diameter of the coupled wheels varied between 5 feet 6 inches and 6 feet, for freight and mixed traffic work respectively.

Maunsell's second basically SECR design was a 2–6–4T intended for fast passenger as well as mixed traffic work. Many parts were interchangeable with the 2–6–0 mixed traffic engines though all the tank engines had 6 foot diameter drivers. One in fact (No. 790) had already been built in SECR days; under Southern auspices a batch was built at Ashford and another by Armstrong Whitworth – eventually Brighton works was also entrusted with the building of a further 10 in 1926. All these engines (K class) were named after rivers. They were used quite extensively on fast passenger trains until the Sevenoaks disaster in 1927, in which 'River Cray' was involved. That raised a question as to their stability at speed, which Walker settled by arranging with Maunsell for the whole class to be converted to 2–6–0 tender engines of class U, when they also lost their names. (The Sevenoaks accident is discussed in Chapter 7.)

Maunsell was undaunted by this experience, to the extent that he sought and obtained authority for the construction of further 2–6–4 engines in class W, with three cylinders, 15 being built between 1931 and 1936. They were, however, confined to freight work, especially cross-London workings, having the 5ft 6in. driving wheels of the N1 2–6–0s, with which most components were interchangeable.

Until a bridge and track strengthening programme (described later) was completed for the Eastern Section, it was still necessary for its principal expresses to continue to be hauled by Wainwright 4–4–0s of the D, E and L classes, sometimes with double-heading. Some relief was obtained when 15 engines, very similar to the L class but with smaller cylinders and 180 lb psi boiler pressure instead of 160, were built in 1926 by the North British Locomotive Company and designated class L1.

In rebuilding the earlier Wainwright 4–4–0s of classes E1 and D1, Maunsell replaced the heavy wheel splashers with a section of raised running plate which gave these fine engines some resemblance to Midland Railway class 2s; perhaps Clayton, the chief draughtsman, had let his Derby background surface here.

Brighton works was, in principle, not intended to be used for new locomotive building. However, Maunsell built there in 1929 a series of eight powerful three-cylinder 0–8–0T locomotives for heavy shunting work, designated class Z, which incorporated Brighton boilers of a design used on the LBSC 0–6–0 class C2/X rebuilt by E. Marsh from R. J. Billinton's C2 class. Some components came from the rebuilt River class.

The second main aspect of Maunsell's initial policy was the development and improvement of the ex-LSWR fleet which included locomotives designed by Urie, Drummond and Adams – and even a contingent, numbering 44 in all, of survivors from the age of the two Beatties, father and son (J. and W. G.), who had been in charge of building for that railway from 1850 to 1877.

Urie's serviceable 4–6–0 passenger express locomotives with

41

exposed motion and high running plates came in two series – H15, built in 1913–14 with 10 examples, and N15 with stovepipe chimneys, built in 1918–23 with 20 examples. In addition, Urie had rebuilt six Drummond 4–6–0s of the E14 and F13 classes.

Maunsell decided to make these basically sound designs the foundation of the Southern's principal passenger locomotive class, the King Arthurs – which finally comprised 74 engines and was Maunsell's biggest single contribution to Southern train running until the Schools class appeared in 1930. The Arthurs were not really a single class, early batches being officially designated rebuilds – a procedure which appealed to Walker, always anxious to keep charges to capital account to a minimum. Only the last batch was classed as new building; 30 came from the North British Locomotive Company and 14 from Eastleigh.

The power and free running of the King Arthurs made them useful for all the Southern's main lines, not just the South Western side. Bridge reconstruction was involved on a large scale; between Victoria and Dover via Tonbridge 21 had to be strengthened, the work being finished in July 1925. One year afterwards the Brighton, Eastbourne and Worthing routes had been cleared for King Arthur use as well as the relief continental route via the Catford loop and Maidstone East. By 1927 the Chatham main line had been similarly treated. The Arthurs used on the Central Section had six-wheel tenders.

These handsome locomotives not merely improved the standard of train running, as many logs in the *Railway Magazine* bore witness, but were a fine publicity asset to the Southern. The glamorous names they bore (the brain-child of John Elliot), of Knights of the Round Table, helped to fix their image in the public mind. They were seen on practically every Southern main line except the Hastings route with its restricted loading gauge.

If the King Arthurs were basically a Urie design, that could not be said of Maunsell's Lord Nelson class of 4–6–0s, of which the first appeared in 1926, a truly original design. It returned to the use of four cylinders, an echo of Drummond practice, but with the angles of the cranks arranged at 135° to give eight separate impulses for each revolution of the driving wheels. That accounted for the exceptionally soft 'beat' of the engine, particularly when starting. The boiler pressure was raised to 220 lb psi and the driving wheels were 6 feet 7 inches in diameter. Maunsell also reintroduced the Belpaire boiler, which had been absent from the Urie designs.

The Lord Nelson class were all built at Eastleigh, and totalled 16. The prototype was given extensive trials before the decision to continue building the class was taken; the subsequent 15 were built in 1928 and 1929.

For a short period in 1926 'Lord Nelson' was classed, on the 'tractive effort' formula, as the most powerful passenger locomotive in Britain, at 33,500 lb. Around that time a competitive spirit had developed, fostered by the Publicity Departments of the four main line railways, leading to claims to possession of the most powerful locomotive in the country. In retrospect, this seems faintly absurd: suitability for the type of train to be hauled, economy and reliability are more important than a theoretical index of power based on particular dimensions which may or may not result in effective performance. That in practice is more likely to result from the characteristics of design of firebox, boiler, valve gear and steam passages rather than wheel diameter, cylinder dimensions and boiler pressure which enter into the 'tractive effort' formula.

The LNER exhibited in the British Empire Exhibition at Wembley in 1924 a Gresley Pacific which it claimed to be one of 'the largest and most powerful passenger engines in Great Britain', although the Great Western's Castle exhibited nearby had a higher tractive effort. The following year the LNER exhibited at the Stockton & Darlington Railway centenary celebrations a Beyer-Garratt 2–8–0 + 0–8–2 locomotive which was (this time correctly) described as 'the most powerful locomotive in Great Britain'.

But publicity was concentrated upon express passenger engines and in 1926 the Lord Nelson was loudly proclaimed the champion. It had a further laurel wreath from the compliment paid to Maunsell by the management of the LMS. That railway was desperately short of a locomotive class suitable for handling the fast and heavy Anglo-Scottish expresses to be introduced with the summer timetable of 1927, including non-stop running between Euston and Carlisle. In fact, there was virtual panic as the date grew nearer and 50 new locomotives were required at short notice. The Great Western, one of whose Castles had been lent to the LMS, was unwilling or unable to help either with workshop capacity or the loan of working drawings (there was no time to start designing from the ground floor up). Maunsell was approached and agreed to lend the Lord Nelson drawings to the LMS and the North British Locomotive Company with whom the order was placed.

The crowning irony was that although the Royal Scot class was a hybrid, including Lord Nelson characteristics and some traditional Midland Railway design features that needed later modification, it performed very well indeed, better in fact than Lord Nelson, which in its first form was inclined to be sluggish. However, the Royal Scot's tractive effort at 33,150 lb was still marginally less than that of the Nelson.

The top position was not retained for long, however, as the Great Western – whose publicity had exploited the virtues of the Castle class very effectively – countered the Southern's publicity by building the King class of 4–6–0s, also by the summer of 1927, with a tractive effort of 40,300 lb (largely obtained by raising the boiler pressure to 250 lb psi), thus effectively overshadowing both the Royal Scot and Lord Nelson classes.

The 15 successors to 'Lord Nelson' were all built at Eastleigh, and a number of modifications were provided on individual engines. No. 857, 'Lord Howe', was fitted in 1937 with a larger, tapered, round-topped boiler instead of the Belpaire firebox, and its steaming power was enhanced by increasing the super-heater surface area. No. 859, 'Lord Hood', was given 6ft 3in. driving wheels instead of 6ft 7in. No. 860, 'Lord Hawke', had a boiler 10 inches longer than its sisters. No. 865, 'Sir John Hawkins', had the cranks arranged at the normal 90° arrangement instead of the 135° of the others. No. 862, 'Lord Collingwood', was fitted with a Kylchap blastpipe and double chimney. Three different types of tender, one six-wheeled and two eight-wheeled – were used in this small class of 16 locomotives.

All these modifications suggested that Maunsell was not satisfied with the performance of the Lord Nelsons and certainly the class, impressive as it was in appearance, lacked the general utility of the King Arthurs. This was partly because they needed a special firing technique to steam well, which only specialist engine crews had mastered.

Maunsell's *chef d'oeuvre* was undoubtedly his 4–4–0 Schools class, of which the first appeared in 1930, named 'Eton'. These fine engines had three cylinders of 16½ in. diameter and 26 in. stroke; the boiler pressure was 220 lb psi and the driving wheels 6 ft 7 in. They were originally intended for use on the Hastings line with its restricted loading gauge, and therefore had round-topped fireboxes instead of the Belpaire type used in the Lord Nelsons, as well as having the cabs slightly cut back, and including tender top sheeting. Thirty of the class were originally built at Eastleigh, but in view of their wide range of usefulness a further ten were ordered in 1934.

They represented the most powerful 4–4–0 class ever to be built in Europe and rapidly demonstrated that they could pull and run with the best. They were drafted all over the Southern from time to time, and showed to great advantage on the difficult hilly routes between Charing Cross and Hastings, and Waterloo and Portsmouth.

The Schools class was one of those happy instances (one cannot say accidents) in which the designer managed to get everything just right. That seems to have happened more often with the classic British 4–4–0 wheel arrangement than with any other. The long catalogue of such types must include Bowen Cooke's George Vs, Holden's Claud Hamiltons, McIntosh's Dunalastairs, Robinson's Directors, Drummond's Greyhounds, and so on.

The Schools boiler was a shorter version of the Arthur boiler, though with a higher working pressure. The grate area and firebox area were unchanged, but the total tube surface was reduced. The use of three instead of two cylinders made it easier to fit the outside cylinders into the Hastings line loading gauge, and it also reduced hammer-blow on the track.

If the Schools had a fault, they were rather more inclined to slip at starting than were the Arthurs; the lower adhesion weight probably made this inevitable.

Surprisingly, in a locomotive class expressly designed to haul

45

moderate loads over a hilly road, the Schools showed up just as well on heavy trains timed at relatively high speeds over more level routes. Cecil J. Allen in 1937 recorded a typical run from Waterloo to Bournemouth Central (108 miles) in $113\frac{3}{4}$ minutes (booked time 116 minutes) with a load of 340 tons behind No. 925, 'Cheltenham'.

Apart from these more glamorous productions, Maunsell built various engines from time to time for general work, including some 4–6–0s for express goods train working – King Arthurs, in fact, with smaller wheels.

An interesting case of conversion of tank into tender locomotives was the rebuilding of the magnificent-looking Baltic 4–6–4 tank engines which L. B. Billinton had built for the principal expresses between London and Brighton. Cecil J. Allen once commented that he had never experienced really outstanding performances by this class, and they suffered from restricted route availability. Their design had taken advantage of the rather more generous loading gauge of the LBSCR as compared with the other constituents of the Southern, and they were therefore confined to that section. As tank engines, too, coal and water capacity was too limited for main line work. They were, incidentally, always run chimney first, involving turning at the end of each trip, making the tank engine formula pointless.

They were rebuilt much on the lines of the King Arthur class, though with larger cylinders (22 inches diameter against $20\frac{1}{2}$ inches) and slightly larger driving wheels (6 ft 9 in. against 6 ft 7 in.). With a lower boiler pressure (180 lb psi against 200 lb) and a slightly lower heating surface, it could be expected that their standard of performance would barely equal that of the Arthurs, which proved to be the case. Cecil J. Allen wrote in 1935 that he had found that the Western Section drivers were not enthusiastic about the rebuilds, compared with the Arthurs. The seven engines in the class were, however, handsome machines and, in addition to retention of the name 'Remembrance' originally given to one Baltic tank as a war memorial, they carried the names of famous railway engineers.

When Maunsell retired in 1937 (at the age of sixty-nine) he left the Southern with a fine fleet of express passenger, mixed traffic and fast freight locomotives. The rapid spread of electrification had removed any need to renew engines that had been built for suburban or country branch line work, since 'cascading' the more modern types displaced by electrification could keep the remoter areas supplied. In consequence, a large collection of elderly but still useful smaller engines could be found all over the system. Connoisseurs of locomotive history had thus a rich field to explore, whilst the important and remunerative traffic was being carried with efficiency on the main lines where steam survived.

Some minor aspects of policy during Maunsell's era need mention. First, no decisive steps were taken to standardise the type of continuous brake. The LSWR had been a vacuum line, the LBSC a Westinghouse one. The SECR had a good deal of dual-fitting, since its two constituents had disagreed over this, as over most other things! The SER had been vacuum, the LCDR Westinghouse. When Maunsell built locomotives intended to have wide availability throughout the system, they were necessarily dual-fitted.

A consolidated numbering scheme took long to appear, but was finally adopted in 1931. It was extremely simple; with the excision of the lettering before the numerals, 1000 was added to the ex-SECR engines and 2000 to those from the LBSCR, the LSWR numbers being unchanged. Engines designated for scrapping had an O prefixed to their numbers, or were numbered in the 3000 series if some continuity of work was expected.

The large numerals on the tender sides lasted until 1940, when the more general practice of displaying them on the cab side was adopted.

The decision about liveries of locomotives and rolling stock was not taken very quickly. Most people would agree that the LSWR green (pea-green rather than apple-green) was more attractive than either the LBSC umber or the SECR's wartime grey. The South Western had also abandoned its brown-and-salmon livery for coaching stock in favour of a darker, Brunswick green. It was an excellent wearing colour, and was used for steam passenger engines when the King Arthurs were delivered from the North British Locomotive Company.

In coaching stock, the constituent railways of the Southern had long been compared unfavourably with the big northern

47

companies. They had a high proportion of four- and six-wheeled vehicles and, especially on the SECR, many long-distance trains were composed of non-corridor, non-lavatory stock. There had been no policy of standardisation and little building of corridor stock except on the LSWR for the Bournemouth and West of England expresses, including both restaurant and 'pantry' cars. The latter, officially classed 'first-class kitchen brakes', introduced a feature which long survived on the Southern, lugs on the side away from the corridor entrance which enabled a table with a folding leg to be set up in compartments so that light meals and refreshments could be served from the 'pantry'. Spare tables, folded, were kept at the end of each coach.

An element of modernity had been introduced with the corridor stock built by Maunsell in 1921 for the SECR principal Continental boat trains. But even the Kent Coast and Folkestone expresses often still incorporated non-corridor stock.

The LBSCR had relied almost entirely upon the inclusion of Pullman cars, which it did much more thoroughly than the SECR, to improve its best trains. Its most impressive carriages were the 'balloon roof' stock built by D. Earle Marsh for the Newhaven boat trains – but even they were non-corridor. These were some first class corridor and saloon coaches running in the 'Stockbrokers' Express, the 'City Limited' between London Bridge and Brighton.

One fruit of Walker's energetic electrification policy was to remove the need to build any new stock for steam suburban services. Maunsell's energies and those of Surrey Warner, who had been brought in from the LSWR to be Assistant Chief Mechanical Engineer (Carriages, Wagons and Road Vehicles), were concentrated upon providing stock for the newly electrified lines, largely by conversion and improvement of old steam stock on the one hand and, on the other, building new corridor vehicles, to an acceptable modern standard, for the principal main line services.

The rolling stock provided for the various electrification schemes is described in Chapters 5 and 9.

Initially, for the Eastern Section, where non-corridor stock was so prevalent, Maunsell and Warner built 58-foot-long corridor vehicles with Buck-eye couplers and Pullman gang-ways. The compartments had side doors. Various batches were built with widths varying between 8 feet for the Hastings line (specially straight-sided, 'narrow' stock was provided here), to 8 feet 6 inches for the Kent Coast and 9 feet (9 feet 3 inches over door handles) elsewhere. Corridor windows in later batches were carried up nearly to roof level to improve visibility, and doors on the corridor side were sited opposite every alternate compart-ment. Unfortunately, a drop-light was provided opposite the other compartments and this often confused passengers, who assumed that there must be a door there.

Several batches of open saloons were built for boat-train and other services, in some cases having, oddly enough, side and not merely end doors. Some unclassified vehicles were built with a wide range of usefulness – officially designated 'nondescripts' or 'N.B.G.s' (though they were far from what the initials might suggest). They were open saloons with 2 + 1 seating along a central corridor and with several side doors. Most important, they had movable class indicator boards fitted into slots outside, and so could be used as first-class vehicles for race specials, second-class for Continental boat trains, and third-class for schools specials and strengthening ordinary trains, sometimes supplementing the restaurant-car seating. Their main use was in the boat trains.

By 1937 the Southern, through a combination of electrifica-tion and building of modern stock for its main line steam-hauled services, had completely transformed its image in the public eye. Maunsell had splendidly supported Walker's policies, and the Southern, from being the least regarded, had good claims to be the favourite main line railway with the travelling public.

While Maunsell is remembered primarily as a successful locomotive designer, the other side of a Chief Mechanical Engineer's work is equally if not more important. Maunsell was both a good administrator and a good production engineer, though admittedly he was well supported by works managers upon whom he could rely to carry out policy decisions. He was loyally backed up by both the works and design staffs. S. C. Townroe has written that Maunsell was 'humble in his unpretentiousness and ready to delegate to his assistants. With these qualities, and an Irish twinkle in his eye, he made an excellent leader.' He was fortunate in having a fine carriage and wagon engineer in Surrey Warner, until the latter retired in 1929. And he was strongly supported by G. H. Pearson as Assistant Chief Mechanical Engineer (Locomotives) and J. Clayton, a design engineer and his personal assistant. Other stalwarts included H. Holcroft, T. S. Finlayson and Leonard Lynes – in total, a very strong team.

Maunsell's office was at Waterloo, well away from all the main works. He inherited control of Eastleigh, Ashford and Brighton, and a carriage and wagon works at Lancing. The workload was of course overwhelmingly that of maintenance – heavy repairs and renewals – though new construction was the centre of public interest.

Eastleigh, relatively modern and well equipped, was a fine legacy from the LSWR. At Ashford Maunsell had already introduced major reforms and the works had a good record; but Brighton suffered from a cramped layout, and was run down from 1931 to 1939. The strategy which Maunsell initially decided upon was to concentrate locomotive construction and repair on Eastleigh and Ashford. New carriage construction would be assigned to Eastleigh, Lancing being devoted to repair of carriages, as well as building underframes for electric stock. Ashford would also construct wagons. Within this general policy, Brighton was given a small amount of new construction as well as repair work from time to time, including building some of the River class 2–6–4T engines which were later converted to tender engines at Brighton, as class U. Later came some further class U 2–6–0 tender engines, and the eight class Z 0–8–0T shunters. (Brighton's capacity was to be revived for war production after 1939.)

The bulk of new locomotive construction was entrusted to Eastleigh, Ashford and the North British Locomotive Company. The pride of Eastleigh was to have built both the Lord Nelson and the Schools classes in their entirety.

Maunsell's time with the Southern probably denied him some of the job satisfaction that his contemporaries on the other three great railways enjoyed. He had little opportunity to turn out large numbers of standard designs, like Collett or Stanier, nor on the other hand to build a wide variety of 'horses for courses' like Gresley. The electrification programme imposed its inexorable limits on investment in steam. The older engines could not just be swept away and replaced; they often had to work on until less antique types, displaced by electrification, could take over their duties. Maunsell's 1923 inheritance of 2,281 engines in 125 classes had fallen to 1,814 in 70 classes by the date of his retirement.

Maunsell's last years were clouded by two illnesses. He had undoubtedly served the Southern very well indeed: within the limits imposed by Company financial policy, he had produced exactly what the shareholders, the management and the rail users needed. And it was kind of Fate to ensure that his last passenger engine was his masterpiece, widely acclaimed.

Chapter 5

SUBURBAN ELECTRIFICATION AND THE BATTLE OF THE SYSTEMS

Undoubtedly the largest single contribution to the Southern's progress between 1923 and 1937, from the bottom of the league table of public esteem to the top, or very near to the top, was its electrification policy. That contrasted vividly with the apparent indifference, or maybe the excessive timidity, in this respect of the other three main lines. Of course the Southern was assisted by its special characteristics – the short average length of journey, the density of traffic in the London area, and the lesser importance of freight – factors which helped to prove the economic justification for investment in electric traction in ways denied to the other lines. Even so, it was a remarkable achievement, largely because the momentum was almost never lost. As one scheme emerged from the paper planning stage into engineering works, the teams moved on to the next task indicated by the General Manager. Relations with the suppliers of electrical equipment – especially English Electric for the motors – were closely maintained, to mutual satisfaction. The whole process was an object lesson in railway modernisation, and one which, sadly, seems to have been forgotten in the years after nationalisation when stop–go reigned.

The planning was supervised and stimulated by a steering committee of Chief Officers, chaired by E. C. Cox. Below it, teams were set to work on the physical details such as the siting of substations, the alterations required to station layouts and signals, the design and siting of rolling stock depots, the design of electrical control equipment, and so on. Rolling stock requirements would be calculated on the basis of a draft timetable and stock working diagrams. The timetable itself would be constructed on the principle laid down by Walker – that passengers dislike having to consult a printed sheet or book and want to use a station much as they would use a bus-stop. That meant (a) 'clock-face' timings, at regular intervals; and (b) no interval between trains longer, usually, than 20 minutes – where traffic justified it, 15 minutes.

The case to be presented to the Board would have to embrace changes in revenue as well as costs. So the traffic receipts at each station would be reviewed and a potential increase under electrification assessed. Loading of trains under existing steam traction would be measured by train counts, and future seating demands calculated. Train miles under steam and future electric traction would be compared and costed. Finally, the effect upon net revenue was ascertained.

Walker was a master of railway financial procedures and had a splendid grasp of figures. He was in a position, which very few General Managers were, to direct the Chief Accountant on the way in which an electrification scheme was to be costed for presentation to the Board. He required every scheme to meet certain minimum targets so far as the Company's net revenue was concerned; the rate of return had to be higher than the current borrowing rate.

However, the Southern did not use the Stock Exchange to raise cash to any substantial extent; all the main line railways experienced difficulty there. There were other sources of finance. One was loans with a government-guaranteed low rate of interest, made available under the Trade Facilities Act; later came the loans from the government-sponsored Railway Finance Corporation at $2\frac{1}{2}$ per cent. Capitalisation of the savings accruing to the Company from the abolition of Passenger Duty – an anachronistic tax levied on fares other than third class – was also a source of finance, especially for the Brighton main line project. But, apart from this, a large part of the outlay on electrification could be financed from reserves, such as the Locomotive Renewal Fund, and by writing displaced steam traction and other equipment out of capital account. Use of second-hand steam carriage bodies and underframes assisted these financial procedures.

It was also on the Southern that the concept of 'sparks effect' was developed – the ability of electrification *per se* to attract more passengers through improvements (sometimes intangible, such as cleaner conditions) in the quality of service. Previously, the general view of electrification held by the main line railways had been that it could be justified only if it reduced working costs. Passengers were assumed to have no interest in the actual type of traction that served them. The Southern's experience proved the contrary.

It would, however, be wrong to think that everything was sunshine from the beginning. Walker inherited two incompatible systems of electric traction already in operation, and a third at quite an advanced stage of planning. The position was:

1   *Ex-LSWR lines electrified at 600 volts direct current, third rail current collection. 660 volts at power station*

	Year opened
Waterloo–East Putney–Wimbledon	1915
Waterloo–Malden–Kingston	1916
Kingston–Richmond–Waterloo ('Kingston roundabout')	1916
Shepperton branch	1916
'Hounslow roundabout'	1916
Malden–Hampton Court Junction	1916
Hampton Court Junction–Hampton Court	1916
Hampton Court Junction–Claygate	1916

2   *Ex-LBSCR lines electrified at 6,600 volts alternating current, 25 cycles (Hertz), overhead wire current collection*

London Bridge–Victoria (South London, or 'Elevated Electric', line)	1909
Victoria–Crystal Palace	1911
Peckham Rye–Tulse Hill and connections	1912

There were also some works started by the LBSCR in 1914, halted on the outbreak of war – the main suppliers of electrical equipment being German – but partially resumed in 1922 before Grouping, for extensions from Balham to Coulsdon North and Sutton. Much less advanced were the former SECR's plans to electrify virtually all its London area network on yet another system, 1,500 volts direct current, with a protected live rail. This had not led to physical works being started, largely because the railway's proposal to build its own power station at Angerstein

Wharf on the Thames had been blocked by the Electricity Commissioners working under the Ministry of Transport. The LSWR had built its own power station at Durnsford Road, Wimbledon, but the LBSCR had purchased its current from the London Electric Supply Corporation, and this was more in line with government policy.

The SECR project was on a big scale; whilst proposing to use multiple-unit trains initially for the suburban services, it envisaged the later use of locomotives for longer-distance passenger and freight trains.

Walker's Chief Electrical Engineer was Herbert Jones, who had been closely associated with the LSWR schemes. But now the Engineer for New Works was Alfred Raworth. Raworth's background had been in industry, followed by a spell with the LSWR, after which he had moved to the SECR in 1918 and had planned that railway's scheme. It helped, that Raworth was a DC rather than an AC man and Walker found him co-operative, though his reputation among the staff was that of something of an autocrat.

One may assume that Walker was from the outset privately convinced that the system he had introduced on the LSWR was the one most suitable for the Southern. But initially he had to cope not merely with Sir William Forbes but also the ex-Brighton element on the Board, and he had to tread warily. The solution was to set up a committee of chief officers under the chairmanship of E. C. Cox to report on the best system to be adopted as the future standard. With this chairman and a New Works Electrical Engineer, both from the SECR, Walker could not be accused of packing the jury with South Western nominees. But he must have been pleased that the Committee recommended standardisation on 600V DC, since this vindicated his personal conviction. However, as a short-term measure the Cox Committee recommended completion of the AC extensions to Sutton and Coulsdon North.

The Board accepted the latter recommendation and took plenty of time to ratify the former one. But eventually, in August 1926, it announced that all future electrification was to be 600V DC and that the Brighton AC network would be converted in conformity.

55

Since in recent years the major electrification schemes on British Railways apart from the Southern Region have been based on high-tension AC current, it is perhaps appropriate to look again at the effects of the Cox Committee's report. The basic virtues of the DC system are, first, the relatively low cost of the third rail compared with that of the overhead wire, its catenary and its supporting structures, whether portal or gantry type. Then, it involves no interference with signal sighting and is easily replaced in the event of disturbance as in the case of a derailment. On the traction side, the DC motor had by 1923 proved reliable and sturdy; moreover, it gave a good power output at low speeds, thus aiding acceleration, which is so important in suburban services with short distances between stops. The disadvantages include the number of substations required, closely spaced, if voltage drop is to be kept within acceptable limits. The third rail offers obvious dangers both to staff working on the line and trespassers or animals straying. It is unsuitable for shunting-yards; and the inevitability of gaps created by points and crossings and road level crossings is a handicap where locomotives are concerned, as they can be stalled (or 'gapped') without traction current. In severe weather ice forming on the rail head may hold up current collection.

A further disadvantage of the live rail is the difficulty of maintaining a perfect alignment – what the civil engineers call a 'top' – on the running rails with hand labour, since the use of tools is somewhat constricted by the need to observe safety precautions.

The Brighton network of AC traction had its corresponding strengths and weaknesses. Among advantages, the use of overhead current collection lent itself to locomotive haulage being introduced so that freight working could be contemplated; and a continuous 'overhead' could be provided in shunting-yards. Track maintenance could be carried out under the same conditions as with steam traction. On the other side, signal sighting could often be impaired by the erection of the 'overhead', and resiting might be involved. Whilst less accessible than the third rail, the overhead wire occasionally led to fatalities, sometimes due to locomotive firemen carelessly lifting their long tools – and contact would be more certain to be fatal than with 600 volts. (It is in fact related that once on Christmas Eve a reveller was found *sitting* on a 600V third rail quite unharmed, owing to being protected by thick woollen underclothing and rubber soles to his shoes.)

One problem with AC is that a major derailment could bring down a substantial portion of the 'overhead' and its supports, which could not be replaced as quickly as the third rail. (This persists on BR today away from the Southern Region.)

Consideration does not appear to have been given to a third possibility, 1,500V DC with overhead current collection, although this was to be recommended as the future standard in Britain by three government committees in turn – the Kennedy Committee in 1921, the Pringle Committee in 1928, and the Weir Committee in 1931. Each, however, agreed that 750V DC with third-rail collection was an acceptable alternative where conditions favoured it.

Outside Britain, overhead current collection was strongly predominant, though with both alternating and direct current, the former especially in Switzerland and Italy.

Walker and Herbert Jones had no doubts about the virtues of DC with third-rail collection; Jones, though a member of the Pringle Committee, had refused to sign its report. The Southern Railway Board, in accepting Walker's view, does not appear to have been concerned by the fact that the Southern was being committed to a system which lent itself chiefly to multiple-unit operation, which was to involve dual traction with steam engines (later diesel) hauling all the freight and some inter-railway through trains over electrified lines. It was to be some years after Walker's retirement before the first DC locomotives were to be built for the Southern, and even thereafter dual traction persisted on quite a large scale.

The high-tension distribution network involved fewer substations than a low-tension system and this helped to offset the extra cost of the overhead structures. Finally, AC traction had the greatest long-term potential for technological development whereas the DC motor had already reached a standard that was to be little improved during the Southern's lifetime, though rotary converters at substations were soon to be replaced by mercury-arc rectifiers and costs were to be reduced once substations could be unattended.

The disadvantages included the rather poor performance of AC motors at that date below their rated normal speed, thus giving acceleration inferior to that with DC motors. The AC National Grid was being standardised at 50 Hz, but this frequency was not suitable for traction equipment and on the Continent either $16\frac{2}{3}$ Hz or 25 Hz were normally used for railway purposes. The later development of DC equipment using the standard 50 Hz frequency could not be foreseen in the 1920s.

While the overhead wire could be continuous in a way impossible with the third rail, low bridges might make it impossible to maintain the clearance above the loading gauge required by Ministry of Transport regulations. In such cases a short 'dead section' of wire had to be inserted – less likely to cause 'gapping' than the third rail but still something of a nuisance.

The other question is whether it was worth converting the AC network to DC in the interests of standardisation. The resources devoted to this could have been employed in extending the total electrified network and thus gaining earlier benefits to rail users. Indeed, many rail users found little if any benefit from the changeover: the LBSCR stock had been generally popular, since it was smoother-riding than the DC sets and was rather less Spartan in its finishings.

Moreover, the last section of the AC network displayed improvements in traction. Motor luggage vans with four 250 hp motors were used in the centre of four-coach sets with the passenger vehicles all trailers or driving trailers – virtually 1,000 hp 'locomotives' working push-pull. They gave better acceleration than the earlier three-coach multiple-units. The first had used motors providing 460 hp; the second series, 600 hp. The power/weight ratio was steadily improving.

The 'last fling' of AC on the Southern had been effected due to the urgent need to counteract the spate of public and press criticism of Southern suburban services in 1923 and 1924. The quickest possible improvement needed to be undertaken and announced. It could best be achieved by a three-pronged attack – by extending the ex-LSWR third-rail system; by resuming work on the ex-LBSCR extensions to Coulsdon and Sutton; and by an early start on the South Eastern side.

The Southern Board approved this programme. Announcing in June 1923 the decision to extend the AC system no doubt helped to placate the ex-LBSCR directors as well as Sir William Forbes. Walker presumably felt that both the urgent need to demonstrate improvements and the money already spent on the project justified temporarily extending a system that he would not wish to perpetuate. Work went ahead quickly and the extensions from Balham to Coulsdon North and from Selhurst to Sutton were opened on 1 April 1925.

Almost simultaneously, the ex-LSWR DC network was extended to Guildford, Leatherhead, Dorking and Effingham Junction. But the most important improvement, and the one that did most to stifle public criticism, was over the former LCDR suburban lines, covering Victoria to Orpington, Holborn Viaduct to Shortlands, and Nunhead to Crystal Palace (High Level). This was quickly followed by the ex-SER lines from Charing Cross and Cannon Street to Orpington and between Lewisham and Hayes, Elmers End and Addiscombe.

These improvements followed the decision to standardise the 600V DC system for the Southern, not merely for new extensions but involving the conversion of the whole AC network. Some economies in operation were calculated, and the package was made more palatable to those who might grumble that conversion was unnecessary by a simultaneous announcement that further sections of the ex-LBSCR lines were to be electrified – on the third rail, of course. They included Streatham Junction to Epsom, Sutton to Epsom Downs, Streatham Junction to Wimbledon, and London Bridge via Forest Hill to Norwood Junction, thus closing a number of gaps in the network. The ex-SECR lines from Purley to Caterham and Tattenham Corner were included.

Would it have made sense to forego the appeal of standardisation and extend the AC system? Inter-working between the former LSWR and LBSCR networks was not very widely developed by the Southern, though Waterloo services were projected from the joint Epsom–Leatherhead line to Dorking North – 4 miles of ex-LBSCR – and Victoria trains

59

from Leatherhead to Effingham Junction, 4¼ miles of ex-LSWR.

A self-contained 'Brighton' network would have involved some problems if the South-Eastern side were DC third-rail. Even so, the Southern transferred the Caterham and Tattenham Corner branches to London Bridge Low Level except at peak hours; the Oxted line was never electrified and the workings over the 'old' main line of the SER from Charing Cross and Cannon Street were vestigial, and steam-hauled in any case. So an incompatible Brighton system would have only limited disadvantages.

With the conversion of the AC network came an extension of the DC system to Dartford by all three routes; the Caterham and Tattenham Corner and Epsom Downs branches obtained the third rail in 1928; in 1929 there was 'infilling' over the Haydons Road–Wimbledon and Streatham Junction–Epsom routes; and in 1930 Wimbledon to West Croydon followed. The march of the third rail seemed unceasing, because Dartford–Gravesend Central came in 1930 and Feltham Junction–Windsor in the same year.

Rather prematurely, the *Railway Magazine* in July 1926 published an article entitled 'Completion of Southern Railway Suburban Electrification'. That work in fact was not to be completed until some main line electrification had been carried out between 1933 and 1939. In a speech in 1933 Walker pointed out that by 1931 293 route-miles and 800 track-miles had been electrified at a total cost of £11·8 million, of which only £6·25 million had been charged to capital.

Electrification had of course involved a great deal more than new trains and a third rail. Cannon Street station and its approaches were completely remodelled in 1926, a remarkable feat of engineering, all carried out between 5 June and 28 June. The new track layout had been set down in a field near New Cross until it could be relaid, section by section, during the period in which the station was closed, platforms altered and colour-light signalling installed.

Rolling stock was largely adapted from existing compartment steam stock, two six-wheeled bodies sometimes being fitted on to a new underframe. This economical procedure had some disadvantages; old-fashioned stock often had an excessive

60

proportion of first-class compartments for modern requirements. The normal make-up was a three-coach unit (motor-
trailer-motor) with a total power of 550 hp. These could be
strengthened as required by inserting a two-coach trailer set
between two motor units. The electric trains carried letters
instead of headlamp codes and passengers were encouraged to
recognise their appropriate letter so as to join the right train. A
famous advertisement in SR compartments showed a collection
of trains (presumably outside a carriage shed) displaying the
brown-bread maker's trademark thus:

> H   (Hampton Court)
> O   (Hounslow and Kingston)
> V   (Kingston Roundabout)
> I   (Dorking)
> S   (Shepperton)

The Southern's commitment to colour-light signalling in
connection with electrification is discussed in Chapter 7.

This huge programme, carried out on 'Walker' principles,
seems to have struck the happy mean between a mere change of
traction on the one hand and complete remodelling of the
railway on the other. Changes needed to facilitate the working of
the much more intensive train service were thoroughly carried
out; on the other hand, what might be considered luxuries – even
though presenting a more modern image – were eschewed. For
instance, the new electric trains served some stations still lit by
Victorian gas lamps. All in all, it managed to combine efficiency
with economy.

When Walker directed the planning team under Cox to turn
its attention to main line electrification, it seemed as though the
outer suburban electrification was complete. That was not really
the case; it had to continue further afield – to Maidstone and
Gillingham in the east, and to Reading in the west. But this
completion came only after Walker's retirement.

Chapter 6

PROGRESS AND PUBLICITY

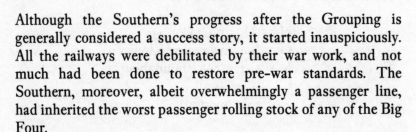

Although the Southern's progress after the Grouping is generally considered a success story, it started inauspiciously. All the railways were debilitated by their war work, and not much had been done to restore pre-war standards. The Southern, moreover, albeit overwhelmingly a passenger line, had inherited the worst passenger rolling stock of any of the Big Four.

Against this, the increase in traffic had been dramatic – 26 per cent more passenger journeys in 1923 than in 1913 – and the peak hour numbers had increased even more, since the peaks had become more compressed. 'Blue-collar' and 'white-collar' workers no longer travelled at such different times in the morning and evening since the general introduction of the eight-hour working day.

It was perhaps unfair of passengers to overlook the Southern's announcements that more electrification had been agreed. But in fact the overcrowding on the steam services was temporarily aggravated by the withdrawal of carriages for conversion to electric working. The public was understandably impatient: five years had passed since the end of the war. There was a general disillusionment with conditions in the post-war world; a coal strike and a railway strike in 1919 had not helped.

Passengers felt entitled to better service, and the main target of dissatisfaction was the ex-SECR system where the electrification planned before the war had not been carried out. Commuters were still riding in overcrowded six-wheelers hauled bumpily along by equally aged tank engines. This was despite the great efforts of E. C. Cox and his staff to improve the operating efficiency and punctuality of the SECR services, where a radical review of timetables and platforming in the congested Borough Market Junction area had led to 'parallel working', with a virtual elimination of conflicting movements between London Bridge, Cannon Street and Charing Cross. But not even better punctuality could eliminate complaints of dirt, discomfort and slowness with outdated steam trains in such intensive suburban services.

By 1924 a virulent press campaign of criticism was being directed at the Southern. Walker's temperament inclined him to concentrate upon effecting improvements, and only when they had taken effect to let the public revise its opinions. But the fierceness of the press campaign could not be ignored; the Board was concerned about it.

Walker was on excellent terms with Lord Ashfield, Chairman of the Underground group. That dated from the war period when Ashfield, then Sir Albert Stanley, had been President of the Board of Trade and, *ex officio*, formal Chairman of the Railway Executive Committee – though Walker as Acting Chairman had in fact performed the duties. Now, the Underground railways were also meeting problems in providing satisfactory service after the war, but they appeared to be almost immune from press criticism. Walker discussed the Southern's predicament with Ashfield, who advised the appointment of someone with specialist knowledge of Fleet Street. Walker agreed and Ashfield proposed the name of J. B. Elliot, the son of one of Fleet Street's great editors, R. D. Blumenfeld of the *Daily Express*. Elliot was only twenty-six but he had already risen to the position of Assistant Editor of the *Evening Standard*, though he was leaving owing to a disagreement over policy.

Walker interviewed Elliot (little imagining that this young man was one day going to sit, successively, in Walker's chair at Waterloo and in Ashfield's at London Transport) and offered him the job. The salary Elliot required, £2,000, caused some eyebrows to be raised in the Staff Section at Waterloo, since it was more than a Divisional Superintendent then received. Elliot also insisted that he should not be regarded as running a specialist department but must be one of the management team, knowing what the policy was, all the time; otherwise blunders and misunderstandings with the press could arise. So it was

63

agreed that he should be called 'Assistant to the General Manager for public relations' – certainly the first use of the term in British business.

Elliot arrived at Waterloo on 16 January 1925, and on 22 January an advertisement appeared in all the principal daily papers, taking the public into the Southern's confidence over the worst problems and explaining what was being done to meet them. Walker had shortly before this addressed a meeting of the Mayors of towns served by the Southern and put up an able defence; Elliot carried this message to the passengers and the public.

It was fortunate for Elliot that he could soon change from the defensive to the offensive. There had been a tendency to keep the planning of electrification schemes under wraps until they could be unveiled by the Chairman at the Annual General Meeting of shareholders. That was nice for the shareholders, but most of the Southern's commuters did not read AGM reports. Now, much more lively publicity was the rule. After a year Elliot's position was to be strengthened when he also took charge of the Advertising Department.

There was plenty of good publicity material. The suburban services were not merely being transformed by the new electric trains; important stations, used by thousands of commuters, were completely rebuilt and modernised. Reconstruction was carried out at Wimbledon, Richmond, Sutton, Epsom, Kingston and Twickenham (the last-named not being completed until after the war), for instance, while less radical improvements were made at many other places.

Entirely new stations for the growing suburban areas were built in apparently endless succession: Motspur Park (1925); Riddlesdown, West Weybridge, Sunnymeads (1927); Petts Wood (1928); Wimbledon Chase, South Merton, Morden South, St Helier, Sutton Common, West Sutton, Hinchley Wood, North Sheen, Chestfield (1930); Syon Lane (1931); Stoneleigh (1932); Berrylands, Woodmansterne (1933); Albany Park (1935); Hersham, Falconwood (1936); Malden Manor, Tolworth (1938); and Chessington North and Chessington South (1939).

New lines that were opened included the Wimbledon–Sutton

line, the Torrington–Halwill light railway, and the Allhallows-on-Sea branch. In the case of the latter, a local developer had laid out a building estate on the south bank of the Thames Estuary. The railway contributed £50,000 to the estate company and appointed a director. The Southern then constructed a single-line branch (doubled later on) from Hoo Junction, which was opened in 1932, with quite a dignified little terminus station. Weekend traffic – mostly day-trippers – could be substantial but the area did not develop as a dormitory for London and the original through coaches to London via Gravesend (two services daily) were soon withdrawn.

An independent project that never came to fruition was the 1925 'Southern Heights Light Railway'. It was intended to run from Orpington to a junction with the Oxted line between Sanderstead and Riddlesdown. There were hopes that the Southern would work this line if it were constructed, but the traffic estimates failed to provide any financial justification for the investment.

Away from the London area, several major station reconstruction schemes were undertaken. Hastings was rebuilt in 1930; Exeter Queen Street – renamed Central – in 1933. Both were substantial architectural works, using brick instead of the concrete employed at Richmond, Surbiton and elsewhere. The façades were dignified but not over-impressive – 'well-mannered' is perhaps the correct adjective to use. Fine, lofty booking halls, almost echoing the work of Charles Holden for the Underground Group, were a special feature. These buildings contrasted with the rather more brash treatment, often called the super-cinema idiom, of the concrete stations. Some stations were rebuilt in a plain, more utilitarian style – among them Woking, Ashford and Haywards Heath. Tonbridge was also modernised, a major feature being a track realignment which raised to 40 mph the speed on the up through line at the bottom of the long climb at 1 in 122 and 1 in 144 to Sevenoaks tunnel – a welcome relief to enginemen.

Ramsgate was a new station on an entirely new site. It again used brick as its principal material, and was the key element in rationalising the Southern system in the East Thanet area. The construction of the Bickley–Chislehurst–Orpington connections in the 1902–4 period had enabled the two SECR main lines to be used in conjunction with any of the London termini. But elsewhere the old separations and duplications persisted. One of the worst was in East Kent, where there were two terminals in both Margate and Ramsgate. The Southern cleared up this situation very effectively by linking the North Kent main line with the Dover–Deal line by a new section of railway, abandoning the old Ramsgate Harbour, Ramsgate Town, and Margate Sands stations, building an entirely new Ramsgate station and rebuilding the former Margate West station. The link railway was about 1½ miles long, with an intermediate station at Dumpton Park. Trains from the Ashford and Dover section could now continue via Ramsgate and Margate along the North Kent line towards Chatham, and vice versa.

Another rationalisation scheme was the construction of new spurs at Lewisham in 1929, which enabled freight from the north via the Metropolitan Widened Lines to reach Hither Green yard without having to pass through the congested London Bridge passenger station, as was the case if the spur at Metropolitan junction was used.

Other routeings which ignored old Company patterns were significant. After electrification trains began running from Waterloo to Dorking (ex-LBSCR) and from Victoria to Effingham Junction (ex-LSWR), and even (for a time) from Victoria to Guildford on Sundays. The Caterham and Tattenham Corner branch trains mostly ran to London Bridge (Low Level) instead of to Charing Cross.

But one attempt at 'rationalisation' introduced early on by E. C. Cox backfired badly. He arranged that the London–Portsmouth services would be concentrated on Waterloo, the Victoria services being severely downgraded. This produced a storm of protest and added to the Southern's unpopularity in 1924. Walker and Cox bowed to the storm and reinstated the through Victoria–Portsmouth fast trains. A rather similar volume of protest was generated by the attempt to concentrate the London–Bexhill services.

The problem of rolling stock for the suburban services was solved by the inflow of electric train sets, some utilising second-hand steam bodies and some newly built throughout. No non-corridor locomotive-hauled stock ever had to be built by the Southern; improved standards on non-electrified branch and secondary lines were achieved by 'cascading' to these services old main line vehicles displaced by new building of corridor stock. On the main lines, the remaining non-corridor bogie stock had to be replaced quickly by new corridor vehicles if the Southern was not to continue to lag behind the other railways. The nominal responsibility for this rested with Maunsell, but the actual design and production lay chiefly in the hands of Surrey Warner, who held the title of Assistant Chief Mechanical Engineer (Carriages, Wagons and Road Vehicles). New up-to-date corridor trains were built for the Kent Coast services in 1924, and in 1925 a standard Southern coach started to be produced in quantity for the West of England trains and also for the Central Section. Restaurant cars were built for the Western Section in 1925, in twin sets (a kitchen-first-class saloon next to a third-class saloon). The Charing Cross–Folkestone and Dover services got corridor stock in 1927, as did the Charing Cross and Cannon Street to Hastings route in 1929 – in this case 'dedicated' stock, only 8 feet wide, to conform to the restricted loading gauge on the route. Further building of vehicles for general use on the Southern followed this progressive treatment of each major route in turn.

It was company policy to create a new, unified, 'Southern Railway' image. In 1924 an official statement asked the staff to refrain from referring to South Western, Brighton and South Eastern Sections and to refer instead to Western, Central and Eastern. A symbolic action was the construction of an opening in 1925 between the two stations at Victoria which henceforth were to be considered a single terminus. A small detail was the general requirement to wear the red neckties formerly included in LSWR uniforms, which (in theory) could be whipped off and used as an emergency danger signal.

Progress was just gathering full momentum when the disaster of the General Strike of 1926 struck. Southern railwaymen joined their comrades on other systems in generally obeying the unions' call to strike in support of the miners. Sir Herbert Walker issued an appeal to the staff to honour their contracts of service, to which some responded. The way in which trains continued to run has become part of the folklore of the strike. Train crews were made up of the few men who defied the unions' call; of management staff, who rolled up their sleeves and took on 'blue-collar' work; and of volunteers from outside the railway, about whom an endless supply of anecdotes, some hilarious, circulated.

The strike lasted from 5 May to 14 May. The number of Southern trains run was:

5 May	338	
6 May	515	
7 May	753	
8 May	868	
9 May (Sunday)	212	passenger and
	62	goods (the latter exceeding the Sunday normal)
10 May	1,069	
11 May	1,370	
12 May	1,636	
13 May	1,655	

On 13 May Sir Herbert Walker announced that men would be re-engaged 'without prejudice to any question that may arise as a result of their having broken their contract of service with the Company'. The unions called for the strike to continue but it was clearly collapsing with the return to work and on 14 May it was settled on terms humiliating to the unions. They signed a joint document with the four main line railways under which the Companies agreed to reinstate men, but only 'as traffic offers', on a basis of seniority at each depot. The unions acknowledged having committed a 'wrongful act' and that reinstatement did not abrogate the Company's right to claim damages for losses suffered. They further promised in future not to instruct their members to strike without previous negotiations, not to support unauthorised industrial action, and not to encourage Special Class men to strike.

Not long after the strike, falling receipts caused the main line Companies to seek a reduction in pay – wages, salaries and directors' fees – which they were able to claim was justified by a fall in the cost of living index. A reduction of $2\frac{1}{2}$ per cent was in force from August 1929 to May 1930 – increased later to 5 per

cent in the case of wages over £2 a week and salaries of over
£100 p.a. These cuts were only restored by instalments as the
worst of the depression lifted from 1933 onwards.

The depression did not damage the Southern quite so
severely as the other groups, largely because its passenger
traffic remained buoyant – in fact, third-class season tickets
increased substantially. But the average fare per passenger fell
from 6s 3¼d (31½p) first class in 1929 to 4s 7¼d (23½p) in 1932;
third class, infinitely more important, fell from 1s 4d (6½p) to
1s ½d (5p). The Southern's net revenue in total fell to a low point
of £4.9 million. That figure incidentally should be compared
with the £7.0 million which the Transport Tribunal created by
the 1921 Railways Act had determined as the 'standard revenue'
which the Southern Railway was entitled to earn.

The Southern practised economy in all its departments. Over
and above this, it discarded – long before Dr Beeching's name
had been heard – a number of sections of railway that were
discovered to be quite uneconomic. Closures from 1929 were:

Line	Year
Tooting Junction to Merton Park	1929
Canterbury–Whitstable (passenger traffic)	1931
Hythe–Sandgate	1931
Lee-on-Solent branch (passenger)	1931
Basingstoke–Alton (passenger)	1932
Bishops Waltham branch (passenger)	1933
Kemp Town branch (passenger)	1933
Chichester–Midhurst (passenger)	1935
Ringwood–Christchurch	1933
Lynton–Barnstaple (narrow-gauge)	1935
Ash Junction–Farnham	1937
Lydd–Dungeness	1937
Devil's Dyke branch	1939
Elham Valley line (by stages)	1940–7

A sad postscript to the closing of the much-loved narrow-
gauge Lynton and Barnstaple line was an auction held on 13
November 1935, when the five locomotives made only between
£34 and £52 each – for scrap. Carriages fetched between £10
and £13 – presumably to be used as hen-houses or garden
sheds. Locomotive nameplates went to the Railway Museum at
York. The signal cabin and the signals at Lynton station sold for
only £7.

A rather more profitable sale of surplus materials was effected to the Gainsborough Picture Corporation, who purchased six elderly coaches and an equally elderly ex-SECR 4–4–0, in order to stage a realistic train crash for the film *The Wrecker*. This was done on 19 August 1928 on the Basingstoke and Alton line, the locomotive being put into full forward gear and the regulator opened just before the crew jumped off; a speed of 40 mph was reached before the collision with a tractor at a level crossing, with gratifyingly realistic results.

Slimming the system by reducing duplicate facilities had been one of the ideas behind the Grouping, but any such steps were as unpopular with the public in the 1930s as they were in the 1960s. Fortunately, the greater part of the Southern network could be considered viable in the days before the explosion of car ownership after the Second World War. Walker's great talent as a manager was to balance his natural pride in improving the service to the public with his duty to protect the shareholders' profits; there was seldom any conflict of interest. The search for economies did not lead Walker, as it had done the dreadful Sir Richard Moon of the London & North Western, to object to any increase in train mileage. On the contrary, Walker believed firmly in frequent services, especially off–peak even where poor loadings might have tempted a reduction in frequency; the 'clock face' facility was the best way to attract new residents who would become season ticket holders. (The American term 'commuter' had not yet displaced the British phrase.)

Among many other innovations must be mentioned the staff suggestions scheme inaugurated in 1925. In the field of innovation, George Ellson, who became Chief Engineer in August 1927 in succession to A. W. Szlumper, had a fertile brain. He designed a spring crossing in which one wing rail was pressed hard against the 'vee' of the crossing to provide a continuous bearing surface for the main line, whilst trains to or from the subsidiary route would force the flangeways open against the spring pressure. He also installed movable diamonds at major turnouts which were unsuitable for spring crossings. In addition, he devised the 'Ellson joint' – an S-shaped end of the rail which, fitted to a matching end, was supposed to eliminate the jolts produced by two butt-ends fishplated together.

70

However, it was not perpetuated, being difficult to machine and expensive for what it offered in improved riding.

Among other excellent developments came the establishment of carriage-washing machines. These served suburban stock at Clapham Junction, Durnsford Road (Wimbledon), Orpington, Selhurst and Slade's Green. The cleanliness of Southern trains owed much to these. Loudspeakers at stations were first introduced in 1932, and two years later news theatres were built at Waterloo and Victoria.

Some relics of the past disappeared. The former LCDR station at Ludgate Hill was closed in March 1929, and the last slip carriage was detached at Hayward's Heath in April 1932.

All the Southern's progressive improvements were brought to the public's notice in highly effective ways. Elliot found in F. V. Milton, an LSWR stalwart who had joined that railway in 1888, a capable assistant. Between them, Southern poster art became highly regarded. The celebrated picture of a small boy looking up at an engine-driver at Waterloo has become part of advertising folklore. But robust advertising based on 'Sunny South Sam' was always effective even if it seemed a trifle crude beside the dignified posters by eminent Royal Academicians displayed by the LMS. The picture of a depressed-looking man 'who needs a holiday on the sunny South Coast' next to one of a jovial individual 'Just back from the South Coast' was typical. The attempt to popularise the East Sussex resorts as 'The Conqueror's Coast' – in connection with the Hastings/ Eastbourne electrification – was perhaps less successful. But literature poured out. E. P. Leigh-Bennett wrote an interesting quarterly pamphlet called *Over the Points* which well matched the GWR booklets such as *The 10.30 Limited*, but was directed more at the commuter than at the dedicated railway enthusiast. *Hints for Holidays* (costing 6d, or 2½p) contained a huge mass of information. All the resorts joined in advertising campaigns, while Elliot himself was tireless in giving staff sales conferences – that is to say, 'pep' talks. Stations were used to display advertising: West Croydon carried on its station canopy a legend 'TO LONDON IN 17 MINUTES: CHEAP TICKETS DAILY'. Such messages were almost standard in the commuter area.

Elliot moved on to become Assistant Traffic Manager (1933),

Assistant General Manager (1937), Deputy General Manager, and, finally, acting General Manager of the Southern, a railway that he had effectively sold to the public. He was succeeded in the field of public relations by Cuthbert Grasemann, who carried on the tradition established by his predecessor. Fortunately, neither Elliot nor Grasemann had ever had to make bricks without straw, plenty of which was always being provided by the Southern management.

Although progress was so unbroken under Walker's firm hand, there were still individual oddities which were, fortunately, never allowed to interfere with the Company's business. F. A. Brant, who had German ancestry, was invaluable to Cox and Walker for his knowledge of Continental traffic possibilities; but he never travelled on former LSWR metals if he could possibly avoid doing so. Equally, Frank Bushrod, the son of an LSWR ship's master, could not stand anything to do with the former SECR and never went abroad in his life. It was common knowledge that Missenden did not particularly favour Raworth, while Raworth and Bulleid, in later years, were always on opposite sides of the fence.

On the other hand, many splendid individuals served the railway without crossing swords with anyone, such as W. H. Shortt, the Western District Engineer based on Exeter, whose track from west of Salisbury into the heart of Cornwall was known as impeccable. He was called in to help improve the Eastern Section permanent way after the Sevenoaks accident, and he presided over two of the Southern's most interesting side-shows. One was the Meldon Quarry near Okehampton, which produced yearly some 200,000 yards of high-quality ballast, vastly superior to the shingle taken by the SECR at Dungeness. The other was the pre-cast concrete factory at Exmouth Junction, which supplied a vast range of items from cable supports to footbridges, fencing, and small prefabricated buildings used all over the system. His reputation extended far outside the railway though he was just one of the 'Southern family' to which Robert Holland Martin used to refer so affectionately.

Chapter 7

SIGNALLING, SAFETY, AND SOME ACCIDENTS

It was perhaps surprising that the constituents of the Southern had all shown, before Grouping, considerable enterprise in signalling developments in ways that might indeed have put some of the wealthier northern lines to shame. The impoverished 'Chatham' had been so impressed by Sykes lock-and-block that it installed it throughout the whole of the busy London area as early as the 1880s – James Staats Forbes showing a praiseworthy concern for his passengers' safety that exceeded his concern for their comfort.

The LBSCR had also come to rely on lock-and-block. Its semaphores were often distinguishable by the height of the masts, intended to provide a sky background. The SECR sometimes avoided using tall masts, especially near overbridges, by painting a white background to the semaphore arm on the bridge's brickwork; and the LSWR sometimes used D-shaped panels mounted on the signal post immediately behind the lower quadrant arm. This practice was abandoned on the Southern, presumably because of the need for cleaning and repainting. 'Brighton' masts had a flat capping shaped rather like a biretta, in contrast to the elaborate finials and spikes of some other railways. The Coligny-Welch illuminated fishtail on distant signals at night was an excellent feature in the days before a yellow distant light was employed. At Victoria, Brighton side, the reconstruction of 1906–8 had included an elaborate system of Sykes electro-mechanical 'banners', circular casings inside which a miniature arm revolved in front of an illuminated ground-glass screen, similar to the 'banner repeaters' used elsewhere but here replacing running line signals to control movement within the station. This installation was replaced by standard colour-lights, with theatre-type route indicators, in June 1939.

The London & South Western's low-pressure automatic semaphore system on part of its main line has already been mentioned. One of its features was the siting of signals on gantries with the semaphores immediately above the track to which they referred. LSWR semaphores were often noticeable for their open latticework steel masts.

Once the Southern embarked upon its programme of electrification, the Signal and Telegraph engineer, W. J. Thorrowgood, (succeeded by Lt-Col. G. L. Hall in 1927), faced a large task in converting the signalling from semaphores to colour-lights where the traffic density was considered to justify this. Such installations were very advanced for their time because usually whole areas were converted instead of providing isolated colour-light signals as distants, which was a practice common on the LMS and the LNER. However, here and there 'islands' of colour-light were provided in semaphore routes, for example at Woking, Guildford, Haslemere, Havant, Dorking, Horsham and Portsmouth Harbour; and occasionally long sections were broken up by intermediate colour-lights controlled by the box in rear.

A key feature was that signals were, as far as possible, brought to the driver's eye level. There were occasional problems here, in that whilst ex-LSWR and ex-LBSCR locomotives were left-hand drive, the ex-SECR engines were right-hand.

The colour-light installations were largely four-position on the Eastern and Western Sections, but usually three-position on the Central. Platform and route indicators were, in the early installations, provided by stencils raised in front of a ground-glass screen illuminated at night; later, theatre-type indicators with lamp bulbs forming letters or numbers came into favour. Originally, splitting signals at junctions, one for each route, had been used but they were discarded in favour of route indicators in the colour-light area after the 1933 Brighton electrification. The routes were shown by a row or rows of white lights above the colour lights; there could be several on a single mast. The first

74

examples came with the re-signalling between Waterloo and Hampton Court Junction in 1936.

Economy generally dictated the retention of mechanical locking alongside the colour-light installations, though motor points were widely introduced to enable signal-boxes to be concentrated. Brighton was the first all-electric locking frame; soon all-electric locking frames were introduced in the major boxes in London, but by 1939 only Woking had been added to Brighton outside the metropolis in this respect.

Right from the start, the Southern's colour-light signalling schemes had incorporated continuous track circuiting, which assisted the extension of automatic and semi-automatic signals, in addition to indicating whether a section of line was occupied or not on the illuminated track diagram in the signal-box.

Another important development was the ability to eliminate conventional block working (with the ringing of bell signals which could be almost continuous in congested areas) by using train describers, indicating class and/or route of train from box to box. These were known on the Southern as 'Walker train describers', after the Telegraph Superintendent of the SER, C. V. Walker, who had initiated the design.

The Brighton electrification in 1933, which provided continuous track circuiting and colour-light signalling from Coulsdon North to Brighton via the Quarry line, saw the introduction of magazine-type train describers which gave the signalman the identity of the next *three* trains approaching him, rather like the London Underground's platform train indicators.

The major new signalling installations in London were triumphs of planning and organisation. Cannon Street was the first, and it was associated with a complete reconstruction of the track layout. The problems of the triangular junction at Borough Market had already been slightly eased by the elimination of the former practice of bringing in trains to and from Charing Cross and reversing them to continue their journey; and there were no longer any Continental departures. But adaptation to the needs of intensive electric train services demanded complete track rationalisation, which was carried out in 1926.

Re-signalling followed at Waterloo in 1936, replacing the famous 'A' box with its 266 levers, dating from 1892. This was a very complex operation, associated with a rearrangement of tracks designed to avoid up suburban trains conflicting with up and down main lines when entering the station. That was achieved by means of a flyover at Durnsford Road, Wimbledon, and alterations at Vauxhall and Clapham Junction following the change from the Up–Up–Down–Down sequence of tracks to Up–Down–Up–Down. The associated colour-light signalling on the main line was mostly three-aspect to Loco Junction (Nine Elms), and four-aspect thence to Hampton Court Junction.

Southern signalling policy was firmly based on the belief that maximum benefit to safety as well as operational efficiency was to be obtained from colour-lights, and that diverting any funds to forms of 'train control', such as the Great Western had installed extensively and the LMS were experimenting with in the 1930s, would be pointless. There was, however, a very brief trial of the Strowger–Hudd electro-magnetic cab signalling system – which found favour with the LMS, and was the ancestor of British Rail's automatic warning system – on the main line at Byfleet in October 1931. It was not installed more widely. On the whole, the Southern's safety record seemed to support this, although it was marred by a few serious accidents.

The first real disaster occurred in 1927, when 2–6–4T No. 800, 'River Cray', was derailed near Sevenoaks, resulting in the deaths of thirteen passengers. The accident raised important questions about both the stability of this type of engine at speed and the quality of the track. Another engine of this class, No. 890, had been previously derailed twice, on 31 March 1927 and 20 August 1927, while 'River Cray' itself had been 'derailed all wheels' at Maidstone East, while running light on 2 August.

On 27 August No. 800 worked the 5 pm Cannon Street to Deal, first stop Ashford. The driver warned his fireman that 'she rolls worse than an L1'. At the country end of Dunton Green station violent rocking occurred, the first pair of coupled wheels having left the road. About 300 yards further on, the leading wheels were also derailed, and the brakes, now fully applied, seemed to have little effect. At a stone-faced bridge with a supporting pillar between the tracks known to enginemen as 'The Dark Arch' the engine struck the bridge abutment, cork-screwed under the bridge and then fell on its side; the train piled

76

up against the engine, and the arch was blocked by the wreckage of the Pullman car 'Carmen'.

An immediate internal inquiry as to the cause was set on foot, Maunsell having to be recalled from holiday. Ellson, the Civil Engineer, maintained that this class of engine was inherently unstable at speed; naturally enough, Maunsell maintained that the track must be at fault. Both could adduce arguments in support of their case. The previous rather ominous derailments pointed to instability, and surging of water in the large side tanks at high speeds was a distinct possibility. On the other hand, the SECR had used shingle ballast from Dungeness, which did not produce adequate stiffening in the permanent way, and in addition the depth of ballast was less than desirable. Contamination by smokebox ash and soil had not improved matters.

Walker delivered a judgement of Solomon: the River class were to be withdrawn from traffic, and converted to tender engines, and the main boat-train route to Dover should be reballasted. Maunsell was partly vindicated by subsequent speed trials of a River class on the LNER main line, when it rode perfectly, while Ellson suffered from the nervous strain of this disaster. W. H. Shortt was called in from Exeter to help to improve the track.

The next year, 1928, on 9 July at London Bridge the driver of a light engine misread a signal and his engine came into broadside collision with a departing train, resulting in two fatalities. Several years later, on 28 January 1933, a similar misreading of a signal within station limits led to an electric train colliding with a goods train at Three Bridges, happily without fatalities. But later that year, on 25 May, there came a serious train accident caused by excessive speed over a section of track under repair at Raynes Park. The derailed coaches were run into by a train on an adjacent track, causing five fatalities.

A worse accident followed on 2 April 1937 at Battersea Park, when a signalman became confused and used his Sykes key to release the locking which enabled him to signal forward the 7.31 am from Coulsdon, causing a rear-end collision with the 7.30 am from London Bridge via Tulse Hill. No fewer than ten fatalities were caused.

77

Accidents and incidents during the Second World War are mentioned in Chapter 18. But in the period between the end of the war and nationalisation several accidents took place. On 10 November 1945 there was a rear-end collision at Woking, leading to thirty people being injured, none fatally. Next year, on 19 March 1946, another rear-end collision occurred in dense fog at Mottingham, a motorman being killed. On Boxing Day in the same year a Weymouth to Waterloo train headed by 4–6–0 No. 851, 'Sir Francis Drake', became derailed at Byfleet. Subsidence of the track was blamed; there were no fatalities.

Lastly, just before the Southern Railway became the Southern Region of BR, three accidents followed in quick succession. On 24 October 1947, in thick fog at South Croydon, the 8.04 am electric train from Tattenham Corner to London Bridge passed Purley Oaks under clear signals and collided with the 7.33 am Haywards Heath to London Bridge which was passing South Croydon Junction home signal at low speed. Once again, a signalman had used the release key of his lock-and-block instrument through a misreading of the situation. No fewer than thirty-one passengers and the motorman of the rear train were killed – the worst tale of fatalities in Southern Railway history.

A fortnight later, on 6 November 1947, the 4.15 pm steam train, Ramsgate to Victoria, collided with the 6.58 pm electric train from Holborn to West Croydon at Herne Hill. The fireman of the steam train had called out 'amber' to the driver after seeing a fogman's lamp signal. At the inquiry the fogman maintained that his lamp had shown 'red' and the Inspecting Officer believed him. One passenger was killed.

Then, on 29 November 1947, there was a rear-end collision at Farnborough, when the 3.05 pm Bournemouth to Waterloo, standing at an automatic signal which had failed at 'danger', was run into by the following 12.15 pm Ilfracombe to Waterloo, whose driver had been told by the signalman at Fleet to pass a signal which also had failed. One passenger and one railwayman were killed.

On the whole, the Southern could claim that its safety record, having regard to the intensity of its electrified services over many congested junctions in the London area, was a good one and justified its policy of relying on three- and four-aspect colour-light signalling to the greatest extent that the available investment funds would permit. Certainly it was an eye-opener to some men from other railways to see how the Southern's drivers would run confidently at full speed through a succession of 'double-yellows' set up by the train ahead. The jigsaw puzzle of the timetable could be performed with deceptive ease – and of course in foggy weather (and any conditions of poor visibility) the colour-light policy paid handsome dividends.

Chapter 8

PLANNING AND COMPETITION IN THE LONDON AREA

———————— ⟩⟨○⟨○⟨⟨○⟨ ————————

Quite unlike the other three grouped railways, the Southern's largest single commercial interest lay in London and the commuter areas of the Home Counties. It was concerned equally with competition for the existing volume of business and stimulation of new business.

So far as competition was concerned, the Southern was, for historical reasons, strongly placed. Grouping had meant that competition between its former constituents had ceased; the most damaging example, that between the SER and the LCDR, had in fact been eliminated almost a quarter of a century earlier. From outside, the main threat had come from the District Railway, which had attempted to push out into the country in much the same way as the Metropolitan Railway was to invade the Chiltern Hills. The District's ambitions had been picturesquely described by the youthful Sam Fay in his history of the LSWR, *A Royal Road*: 'Tired of burrowing like a mole in the bowels of the great City, [the District Company] cast their eyes enviously upon the fair and rich traffic of the South Western suburban system.' In fact the District had set its sights on two prime traffic objectives, Windsor and Guildford. It had been bought off or fought to a standstill by compromises which eventually gave it running powers enabling it to reach Wimbledon and Richmond via two subsidiary routes of the LSWR.

Over on the south-east side, the Metropolitan Railway ran via the East London line to New Cross (both stations) but that was all, apart from the extension of the City & South London tube to

Clapham Common and the much shorter projection of the Bakerloo tube to Elephant and Castle.

A glance at the Underground railway map in 1923 shows a big concentration north of the Thames, with lines radiating in every direction – though principally north, north-west and west – but south of the river very little, only the short sections mentioned. Underground extension had been discouraged by the keen interest shown by the Southern's constituent companies in short-distance and commuter traffic, which was not shared by the other main lines, apart from the Great Eastern. The Great Western, the London & North Western and the Midland attached comparatively little importance to suburban traffic, which might get in the way of their expresses, while the Great Northern had tried to reduce the occupation of King's Cross Station by allowing the North London Railway to siphon off quite a lot of its commuter business.

But at Waterloo and London Bridge the attitude was different. Railway profitability depends on volume business and south London offered this, so that a great network of suburban lines – a real cat's cradle – had been developed without leaving untouched the areas of virgin territory that the Underground had been unable to exploit north of the river.

One serious and potentially dangerous clash with the London Traffic 'Combine' came just after the Southern had been formed, in 1923. It was over the extension of the City & South London tube to Morden, part of the creation of the Northern Line as an amalgamation of the Hampstead tube and the CSLR. The Underground group proposed to link this extension with a dormant scheme, sanctioned by Parliament in 1910, for a new railway from Wimbledon to Sutton. This had been originally promoted by an independent company which had hoped to make advantageous terms – working, leasing, or sale – with one of the two major railways, the LSWR and the LBSCR, which it joined at its extremities. Having failed to achieve this, it managed to dispose of its powers, with parliamentary consent, to the District Railway in 1912. Construction had not started before the war, however; and the Underground extension was now planned to put it in hand and also effect a junction with the extension of the CSLR, at Morden.

81

The Southern Railway opposed both the granting of powers to extend the tube from Clapham Common and the Wimbledon–Sutton connection; but, as the result of horse-trading between Sir Herbert Walker and Lord Ashfield, a bargain was struck whereby the Wimbledon and Sutton powers were transferred to the Southern Railway in exchange for the latter withdrawing its opposition to the Morden extension. The proposed junction of the two lines was abandoned. The Wimbledon–Sutton line was actually built, but in no great hurry, by the Southern, not being opened until 1930.

As regards the competition from road services, there was an extensive tramway network, including the systems of the London County Council, Croydon Corporation and other councils, as well as the BET group's South Metropolitan Electric Tramways, which competed for short-distance ridership.

However, just as the LBSCR's electrification of the South London line had won back traffic lost to the trams, the Southern's electrification must have had a similar effect, though it cannot be exactly measured. The growth in rail passenger journeys came from a combination of causes, including housing development and rising incomes.

The bus network was basically that of the London General Omnibus Company, part of the 'Combine' presided over by Lord Ashfield. However, soon after 1923 the 'pirates' began to operate in London, tending to 'cream' the traffic by concentrating on the more profitable routes and the more profitable times of day.

In the early 1920s a measure of competition appeared from the General which had been gingerly pushing services out into the country, largely to cater for pleasure traffic. For instance, Route 105 (Ealing to Surbiton Station) was extended to Leatherhead on Sundays. An even longer penetration into rural Surrey was by Route 107 (Clapham Common to Dorking). Expansion into Southern Railway territory was further stimulated by the enterprise of A. H. Hawkins, who, starting with a one-vehicle Redhill–Reigate service, built up a country bus network under the name of East Surrey Traction Company and then negotiated an agreement with the LGOC which led to the formation of London General Country Services. This was the forerunner of London Transport's 'green bus' network, and also of its Green Line Coaches, which initially posed a real threat to the Southern, since they ran from central London to Gravesend, Wrotham, Tunbridge Wells, East Grinstead, Crawley, Dorking, Guildford, Woking, Chertsey and Windsor. The attraction of the coaches was based on price and convenience – not speed; the coaches were much slower than the trains. The competition thus chiefly affected rail off-peak travel, rather than daily commuting.

However, the formation of the London Passenger Transport Board in 1933 took the sting out of competition owing to the setting up of a statutory pool of receipts from passenger traffic within the Board's area. These, after deduction of working expenses, were shared between the LPTB and the main line railways. The LPTB had, in round figures, 62 per cent of the total; the Southern had 25½ per cent – much the largest share (as one would expect) of any of the main line railways.

As regards the creation of demand, the freedom that the Southern enjoyed in the 1920s contrasts vividly with the situation today. There was no Green Belt; developers could buy land and cover it with new houses wherever they pleased, sometimes with aesthetically deplorable results. Thousands of acres were covered with small semi-detached houses, often of a depressing similarity, but into which people moved gladly as a welcome alternative to crowded and expensive inner-city lodgings. The Southern cashed in energetically on the development of this suburban sprawl and encouraged its spread into the Home Counties with the advertising slogans 'Live in Surrey, Free from Worry' and 'Live in Kent and Be Content'. In 1929 it issued several booklets – *The Country at London's Door* and *Southern Homes*.

Developers entered into a partnership with the railway over the building of stations that would make new housing estates more attractive to intending commuters. At Hinchley Wood the developer contributed £2,500 towards the cost of a station and also bought Southern Railway stock which he agreed to forfeit if 150 houses were not built within three years. At Berrylands, 90 per cent of the cost of the new station (£6,275) was met by seven building firms. Subsidies were also obtained for new stations at Hersham and Woodmansterne.

It must be said that, whilst the unplanned suburban sprawl of London in the 1920s and 1930s nowadays looks rather like a planning disaster, its worst aspect – 'ribbon development' along main roads – was not stimulated by the railway. Clustering of new houses around a station, or 'nodal' development which fostered the provision of shops, pubs and other amenities, was infinitely preferable to the long, thin ribbons of houses far removed from any social centre which had originally sprung up with the extension of bus and tram routes and which eventually were to become chiefly dependent upon the motor car for any kind of social life.

It was a long, slow process before the Green Belt concept arrived to hinder the activities either of developers or of the railway. The London Society had campaigned for it over many years, but it only began to take shape in 1935 with the London County Council's Green Belt Scheme, later made statutory by the Green Belt (London and Home Counties) Act of 1938. That fell far short of the comprehensive planning controls instituted by the Town and Country Planning Act, 1947, but its effect was to induce the Southern to cut back its projected new line from Motspur Park to Leatherhead ($7\frac{1}{2}$ miles) at Chessington South, just over half-way. Overall, however, the close social inter-relation between transport and land use had scarcely been appreciated in Southern Railway days. The nearest approach was when railway Private Bills were examined by parliamentary committees and witnesses were enabled to express their views as to the desirability, the necessity and the effects of railway proposals for new works.

However, one major encounter between the Southern and planning bodies did take place over the Charing Cross railway bridge. It was sparked off by the discovery that Rennie's Waterloo Bridge had subsided and needed rebuilding. The whole question of cross-river road traffic then began to occupy attention. A Royal Commission on the subject set up in 1926 reported in favour of a new road bridge at Charing Cross. The LCC sought powers to construct this in 1929, on the basis that the Southern Railway would build a new terminus on the south

20 'Bull-nose' electric stock at Hounslow

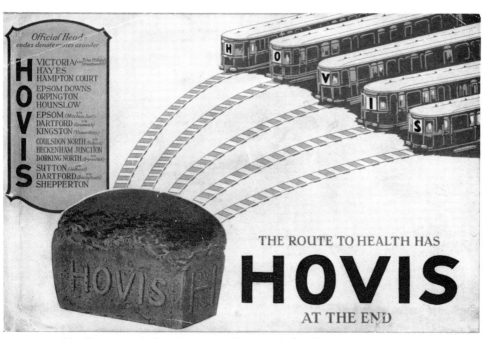

21 Brown bread advertising, capitalising on the Southern's route indicators!

22   The 'Bournemouth Belle', headed by a 'Nelson' class no. 852, 'Sir Walter Raleigh'

23   The 'Golden Arrow' had lost some of its original glamour when it ran as only a
Pullman portion of an ordinary boat train. The train is passing Shortlands Junction in 1939
hauled by 'Lord Nelson' no. 863 'Lord Rodney'

4   Frequency was a well-publicised feature of the electric services

25   One wonders how long this idyllic countryside would remain untouched after the commuters had arrived in quantity!

26   Semaphores galore, at Lewes

27 'King Arthur' class, no. 783 'Sir Gillemere' near Brookwood on a down Bournemouth train

28 The standard position–light junction route–indicators which replaced splitting signals in later years.

29 A section of the Waterloo signal box, showing miniature lever frame, in 1937

30 The Southern's safety record was good; but this is one reminder of what followed the derailment of 'River Cray' near Sevenoaks in 1927

31   The result of the Battersea Park accident in 1937

32   A good example of 'Southern Odeon' architecture – Malden Manor on the
Chessington branch

33 Inaugural day at Victoria of the electric 'Southern Belle'

34 A 6PUL Brighton set passing Merstham in 1937

35   Interior of First Class compartment (4COR set) for Portsmouth services

36   The Newhaven boat trains remained steam-hauled – in this case double-headed by a
'B1' and an 'H2', passing Clapham Junction in 1939

bank on the site of the present Festival Hall. Charing Cross railway bridge and station would be demolished and replaced by a new road bridge. The government refused to make the 75 per cent grant towards the cost, which included reimbursing the Southern Railway for its outlays, plus £325,000 compensation for disturbance. Although the Southern had agreed to accept this proposal, it fell through in the absence of government support.

In 1933, temporarily abandoning the Charing Cross proposal, the LCC started to rebuild Waterloo Bridge. While this was in progress, the statutory London and Home Counties Advisory Committee reported in favour of a new Charing Cross bridge with approach roads stretching from the Euston Road in the north to the Elephant and Castle and St George's Circus in the south. It was to be a combined road and rail bridge – vastly expensive, and the LCC refused to support the project on the ground of cost. Deadlock ensued once more.

In 1935 the Secretary of the Advisory Committee returned to the subject and asked Walker for his views on the removal of Charing Cross station to the south bank. Walker replied that the Southern would not object to a new combined road and rail bridge but felt that moving the station would 'be to create and not to solve, a traffic problem', in view of the inconvenience to passengers who used Charing Cross – 103,478 daily, on average in 687 trains, in 1935. The stalemate has continued ever since. The railway bridge may be an aesthetic disaster but not a social planning one.

The Southern participated in the benefits all the main line railways received from the government-sponsored 1935–40 New Works Plan, designed to reduce unemployment by financing railway improvements at a low, government-guaranteed rate of interest. This money was applied mainly to electrification schemes. The SR did not, however, share in the companion scheme for London, of which London Transport took approximately a 70 per cent share, the LNER 25 per cent and the GWR 5 per cent. The government view was that the urgent needs for improvement in London's rail facilities lay north of the Thames, an implicit compliment to the Southern's progressive past policies!

However, within the Standing Joint Committee organisation some independent and very interesting projects were examined before the war, J. L. Harrington being the Southern's active representative. One was for an extension of the Waterloo & City tube, either to an end-on junction with the Finsbury Park–Moorgate tube of London Transport, or alternatively to link up with the East London line. The former was dropped owing to engineering problems in the Bank area, the second from insufficient traffic prospects. Another project that looked promising was an extension of the Bakerloo tube from Elephant and Castle over the Southern's Bexleyheath route to Dartford, which would in part have run alongside the Catford loop to Nunhead and then via Blackheath. If carried out, it would have eliminated the long-drawn-out controversy over extending the Bakerloo Line in the 1950s, which ended in deadlock.

In the last years of the Southern's existence a series of ineffectual suggestions were made as part of the 'post-war planning' process. They appeared in the brief passages about the railways in the 1943 Abercrombie Report and the County of London Plan, in which wistful references were made to the desirability of eliminating surface railways from central London. Klapper comments acidly that these seemed to assume that 'the viaduct railways of South London were an evil influence and cut one district off from another, but this would be put right by a network of viaduct roads which would replace them. Alas, this generation has seen West Way as a viaduct road which harms the environment.' Sir Herbert Walker would, had he still lived, have commended Klapper's words.

Chapter 9

MAIN LINE ELECTRIFICATION: WALKER'S CROWNING ACHIEVEMENT

When Walker made his celebrated announcement in 1929 to the Traffic Officers Conference, 'Gentlemen, I have decided to electrify to Brighton', a slightly sour reflection might have crossed the mind of any former LBSCR man. It would have been that if, three years previously, it had not been decided to convert the AC network to DC, by 1929 the electric trains could have already been running to Brighton. And, if locomotive traction had been included, the engines that provided the fast passenger services in the daytime could have hauled the freight at night, an economical arrangement, reducing the amount of steam traction.

However, since so much weight had been attached to the convenience of having one standard system, it followed that the limitations of the third rail had to be accepted. In effect, this meant that fast long-distance trains must be multiple-units, very similar to the suburban stock in operating characteristics, but offering superior passenger comfort – corridors, gangways and lavatories, with access to catering vehicles where these were provided.

The Brighton scheme extended as far as West Worthing, where carriage cleaning facilities were sited. Colour-light signalling was installed from Coulsdon North to Brighton. Haywards Heath station was remodelled with two island platforms, and a main electrical control room was built at Three Bridges. Outside Brighton the curve leading direct to the West

Coast line at Hove was also electrified, as was the short length from Redhill to Reigate. Originally the whole line from Redhill to Guildford had been included in the outline scheme, but it was soon dropped beyond Reigate as lacking sufficient traffic justification.

The sets for the fast services were composed of five coaches (two motor and three trailer) and a first- and third-class composite Pullman, designated 6 PUL. The total horsepower was 1,800 in each unit; two units ran, coupled together, for the heavier-loading services, making a twelve-coach train with two catering vehicles. However, the character of the famous 'City Limited' was preserved: the 8.45 am ex Brighton and the 5 pm from London Bridge were worked with special sets incorporating no less than three first-class trailing vehicles in each unit.

The most publicised stock, however, was the all-Pullman electric replacement for the steam-hauled 'Southern Belle' (renamed 'Brighton Belle' in 1934). Three five-coach units were built – code name 5 BEL – and two were normally worked as a ten-coach train, with one unit spare. In accordance with Pullman practice, in each unit the two first-class cars were named, but the three third-class cars were only numbered. It has been commented that the names given nicely reflected the fashionable girls' names of the 1930s – Hazel, Doris, Audrey, Vera, Gwen and Mona. (Mona Lott had not yet become a well-known character in a radio series, or Pullman managers might have had second thoughts.)

The semi-fast trains were provided by four-car units, three cars being compartment vehicles with no corridor, and one a composite corridor vehicle with two lavatories – 4 LAV code. The stopping services were covered by non-lavatory two-coach units, appropriately coded 2 NOL.

The rolling stock was of solid wood-and-steel construction, typical of Maunsell. The express units were powered by traction motors of broadly similar design to those for the suburban stock, but geared to give a higher balancing speed on the level and a higher maximum safe speed downhill, though with lower acceleration.

The Brighton electric timetable reflected all Walker's principles: a non-stop in 60 minutes, with semi-fasts and stopping trains, totalling six every hour, in each direction – four to or from Victoria, two to or from London Bridge. The fast service ran up to a midnight departure from Victoria; some of the hourly 'slots' were taken up by 'Belle' workings. There were of course extra peak-hour trains and the 'City Limited' retained its traditional 8.45 am start from Brighton.

Brighton commuters welcomed the comprehensive new service but quite a number found the riding of the electric stock less comfortable than that of the displaced steam stock. In fact, complaints were received about the rough riding over points and crossings at places where lower speeds had been customary in the past. It was a new experience for the Southern motormen to have so much power under their hand on the controller, and some found this a little too exhilarating!

Within its limitations, the Brighton electrification was undoubtedly a success, from its opening on 1 January 1933. Some people suggested that the change of traction ought to have produced a quicker journey than with steam, which undoubtedly was possible – 'net time' from London to Brighton could be as little as 47 minutes if trains were delayed and then had to make up time. But, although the working timetable showed some timings in less than 60 minutes, the standard hourly schedule was felt to be a commercial advantage and it was rigidly adhered to in the public book.

Surprisingly, Walker did not have an easy time with the Southern Board when he proposed electrifying the Eastbourne and Hastings services. On the face of it, the case was cast-iron. It would eliminate quite a lot of steam traction over electrified lines; the cost was under £1·8 million, with half coming from internal reserves. Worthwhile savings in operating costs were forecast. But the Board had a tradition that decisions must be unanimous; if even one director jibbed at a proposal it would be deferred for further consideration. That happened with the Eastbourne/Hastings scheme, which was first proposed in May 1932, deferred and resubmitted as amended in June 1933, deferred again and finally approved in November 1933. This was the first real setback to Walker's policy of maintaining a rolling programme which kept the whole electrification team, or rather teams, together and fully employed.

The Eastbourne/Hastings project followed the general lines of the Brighton electrification. But one important change reflected the fact that the Pullman Car Company had found it difficult to finance the purchase of the 15 new cars for the 'Belle' plus the 23 single cars for the 6 PUL units; deferred payments had had to be arranged with the builders, Metropolitan-Cammell. So for the next group of services about half the units included 'pantry cars' which were staffed by Pullman but built by the Southern, and for which no supplement was charged in the catering area. In Pullman terms they were ROVs – railway-owned vehicles. The Southern code for the units was 6 PAN. However, they often worked in conjunction with a 6 PUL set and thus passengers had a choice of catering facilities – though splitting the two units for different destinations might restrict this.

The Eastbourne and Hastings scheme came ten years after the idea of 'rationalising' the two routes to the latter town by concentrating upon the Charing Cross line had run into fierce opposition, similar to that aroused by the attempt to concentrate the Portsmouth services on Waterloo.

The third rail was carried beyond Hastings as far as Ore on the Ashford line, to reach a carriage stabling depot. It also included Seaford and Newhaven, but the boat trains to Newhaven Harbour continued to be steam-hauled – often by Marsh Atlantics – apparently on account of the need to include luggage vans and occasionally strengthening vehicles.

The next major project, authorised in July 1935 and opened on 1 July 1937, was the Portsmouth 'No. 1' scheme. It embraced electrifying from Hampton Court Junction to Woking, Guildford and Portsmouth and from Woking to Pirbright Junction and Farnham. The loop from Staines to Weybridge and West Weybridge (now Byfleet and New Haw) was also included.

The timetable was of course based on the 'clock-face' principle. There were fast trains to Portsmouth Harbour every hour, calling at Guildford, Haslemere and Portsmouth & Southsea en route. Extra trains on a different pattern – all stations from Guildford – were provided in the peak hours. They, as well as the standard fasts, had catering facilities, though not Pullman cars.

Stopping services were non-stop from Waterloo to Surbiton, then all stations to Woking, where they divided; one portion ran to Farnham and the other to Portsmouth. The latter was overtaken by the fast services at Guildford where interchange was achieved.

Incidental benefits to passengers came from the rebuilding of Woking and Havant stations. Guildford had not yet assumed the extreme dilapidation into which it sank after the war, otherwise it might well have been included.

Instead of the six-coach sets without gangway connections at their outer ends built for the Brighton and Eastbourne trains, Maunsell and Raworth provided four-coach sets with centre gangways at each end, the motorman's compartment being compressed to one side and closed off when the gangways were connected up for through communication between units. Such through communication was needed, of course for access to the catering vehicles. There were two types of unit, one including two motor open-saloon thirds, one compartment third, and a compartment composite carriage. It was coded 4 COR. The other type of unit comprised the same pair of motor coaches, but in between were two catering vehicles, a kitchen/open third and a first compartment carriage with a small dining saloon. These units were coded 4 RES. The catering was provided by Frederick Hotels, who had by this time taken over from Spiers and Pond on the Western Section.

The staff promptly nicknamed these trains 'Nelsons'. One reason was that they started or finished their journeys within sight of the masts of the *Victory* at Portsmouth; another, that the service numbers displayed at one side of the centre gangway gave an approaching train a 'one-eyed' appearance.

The 'Nelsons' totalled 2,700 hp for a twelve-coach train, less than the 3,600 hp for a Brighton set. This was surprising in view of the much steeper gradients on the Portsmouth direct line, 1 in 80 up to the summits at Haslemere and Buriton tunnel, compared with the easier ruling gradient (1 in 264) of the Brighton main line. The Schools class had been performing some excellent feats of haulage in 90-minute timings between Waterloo and Portsmouth & Southsea; the 'Nelsons' did not improve on this overall, but they did include two intermediate stops. The standard Haslemere stop was perhaps surprising in view of that town's size, but it assisted in stimulating season-ticket sales on quite a large scale and a substantial residential hinterland was served.

The 'Nelson' stock was notorious for rough riding, especially round the curves on the Guildford–Havant section of the line. The gangways at the front of the train also waggled disconcertingly from side to side at speed. On summer Saturdays fast trains for the Isle of Wight were added to the regular service, some non-stop to Portsmouth, but all with restaurant cars. The same train crews and the same rolling stock thus catered for daily commuters, inter-city business travellers between Portsmouth and London, and holidaymakers – a highly economic arrangement.

'Portsmouth No. 1' was soon followed by 'Portsmouth No. 2' – really a misnomer, since Bognor and Littlehampton were the main beneficiaries from this scheme. It included the Mid-Sussex line from Dorking North via Horsham to Ford, and from West Worthing to Ford, Chichester and Havant (for Portsmouth), with the Bognor and Littlehampton branches. Like the Portsmouth No. 1 project, the finance came largely from the Railway Finance Corporation, with a low rate of interest obtained by a Treasury guarantee given on the basis that railway new works would help to relieve unemployment.

The trains, which normally were divided or made up at Barnham between a Portsmouth and a Bognor portion, were made up of 4 COR units and 4 BUF units. In the latter, Oliver Bulleid, who had now replaced Maunsell, let himself go (though the Chairman is supposed to have taken some part) as regards the interior design of the buffet cars. There were no windows – presumably lest attention should be distracted from the serious business of drinking – in the bar portion, which included bar stools. In the feeding area the tables faced outwards but they had curious concave areas scooped out of them to increase gangway space whilst similar 'scallops' distinguished the interior door-frames and partitions. It was all calculated to worry a reveller returning home after a long evening in London and seeking a nightcap or two before leaving the train.

The service greatly improved Bognor's communications with

London, like those of Arundel, Pulborough and Horsham. Littlehampton was served by trains down the main line taking the Hove curve.

Consideration was given from time to time to electrifying the Horsham–Shoreham line via Steyning; it was a useful potential diversionary route in the event of the main line being blocked, but the traffic justification was slight. (It was sometimes used for Sunday excursions to Brighton from places as diverse as Sutton and even Guildford.) Similarly, the Oxted line to East Grinstead and Tunbridge Wells West never saw the third rail; one reason adduced for this was the absence of any parallel main road facilitating coach competition.

With such achievements behind him, it must have been a severe disappointment to Walker that the last major submission he made to the Board before his retirement, to electrify the ex-SER Hastings line – involving the Sevenoaks–Tunbridge Wells–Hastings and Crowhurst–Bexhill West sections – was turned down.

The Board's timidity seems extraordinary today. All previous projects had fulfilled the expectation of increased receipts, over and above what was needed to meet working costs and the interest on capital. The Hastings scheme went into limbo until after the Second World War, when the Southern's Post-War Plan revived it. Under nationalisation it was again put aside in favour of diesel multiple-unit trains. At long last, in May 1986 (almost half a century after Walker's attempt to get the third rail laid), electric trains began running between Tonbridge and Hastings.

Walker will always be remembered for what he achieved, often on a shoestring. Had he had a slightly more courageous Board, he would not have lost a single project.

Chapter 10

FROM WALKER TO WARTIME

Walker's retirement on 14 October 1937 marked the end of an era for the Southern. With him Edwin Cox and R. E. L. Maunsell also retired; and it was not merely a generation of managers that changed. Frank Dudley Docker, who had been a staunch supporter of Walker on the Board, and whose approval had often been vital to securing Board unanimity over, for instance, electrification, also retired. Although it was not stated publicly, it was generally understood that he did so in order to create a vacancy which Walker could fill. Certainly, Walker was promptly elected a Director on his retirement, an honour he much appreciated.

Walker also was appointed to one or two other Boards, including The United Steel Companies Ltd, a very important supplier of railway materials to the Southern. Its Workington steel works rolled rails of high quality from the acid steel produced from the local haematite iron ore; the rails came coastwise to the Southern Railway's Angerstein Wharf on the Thames, which was cheaper than having them carried as rail freight by the LMS from Workington to London!

When Walker retired it created no surprise in railway circles that he should be succeeded as General Manager by Gilbert Szlumper. Szlumper had trained as an engineer, but he had had intimate experience of docks and marine work and also of railway administration at the top level for a long time as Walker's Assistant. He was not a traffic man, but that side of the railway had been well sewn up under Cox and now was entrusted to the capable hands of Eustace Missenden.

But no one could have expected that Szlumper's occupancy of

Walker's chair at Waterloo would last less than two years. He was very much one of the 'Southern family'. After his death, Elliot wrote in *The Times* that Szlumper was 'a man of shining integrity ... an individualist himself, he gave his colleagues a great deal of freedom to do their work in their own way and inspired them at all times by his energy, enthusiasm and complete absence of pomposity. Fools and knaves had no chance with him, and his gusty sense of humour was a byword in the world of railwaymen everywhere.'

Obviously Szlumper would have to leave more to his Traffic Manager, Missenden, than Walker had done to Cox, but the Southern could be said in 1937 to be coasting along on the impetus imparted by the Walker-Cox regime. Szlumper was beginning nevertheless to show that he would be a fine General Manager, given a little time. Meanwhile a number of Southern stalwarts of the Walker era were being replaced by new names.

The most striking arrival was Oliver Bulleid from the LNER to succeed Maunsell as Chief Mechanical Engineer. Below the CME, Leonard Lynes was now in charge of carriage and wagon matters, though he did not have quite the status formerly enjoyed by Surrey Warner until the latter's retirement in 1929, that of Assistant Chief Mechanical Engineer. H. Holcroft matched Lynes on the locomotive side, both being designated Technical Assistants. Herbert Jones was followed as Chief Electrical Engineer in 1938 by Alfred Raworth, and A. D. Jones had retired in 1936 as Locomotive Running Superintendent, being succeeded by Alan Cobb.

Frank Bushrod, who had been Cox's right-hand man on the operating side since the Traffic organisation was set up, had retired in 1935 and was followed first by H. E. O. ('Toby') Wheeler and then by S. W. Smart.

In 1939 the nonagenarian Charles Sheath retired from the Board after a railway career that had started in 1864 under a chief, Samuel Smiles, who had been a friend of George Stephenson! He died in the following year.

Walker's programme of electrification continued to roll during Szlumper's years. It was almost a routine matter when the 'Portsmouth No. 2' project was completed, nine months after Szlumper took over, and then the third rail was extended on the

Western side to Reading and to Guildford via Ascot, opening on 1 January 1939. Just six months later the third rail reached Maidstone West from Gravesend, Gillingham from Swanley and Maidstone East from Otford. The familiar principle of serving two destinations with 'splitters' was carried out by dividing and making up sections of trains at Swanley and Ascot. Swanley station was completely remodelled with two island platforms, on a new site just east of the junction. These works, incidentally, were the last to be financed by the Railway Finance Corporation's programme designed to relieve unemployment. The total cost was £1 million for the Reading–Ascot complex and £1·75 million for the Kent extensions. Clearances on the North Kent line had to be increased to allow of standard SR 9-foot-wide stock being used.

By this time the Southern's suburban rolling stock no longer looked very modern. The LNER was planning its Liverpool Street to Shenfield electrification (not completed until after the war) with open stock and power doors. But the Southern operators adhered strictly to swing doors and compartments as offering the maximum number of seats – although this caused extreme passenger discomfort whenever standing took place. The London Underground's views of carriage design had no place in Southern thinking.

On the main lines, the Operating Department was exploiting to the full the splendid capabilities of the 40 Schools class engines. Designed originally for the Hastings route, they had done equally well on the Waterloo–Portsmouth line until replaced by the 1937 electric sets, when they were put on to the Bournemouth line, where they performed remarkably well with heavier trains than they had been designed to haul.

There was, however, a need for more modern rolling stock: Surrey Warner's main line carriages of the 1920s were beginning to look outdated by comparison with the most recent stock on the LMS or the LNER. It has been suggested that it was Bulleid's long experience of carriage and wagon work, even more than his novel ideas on locomotive design, that made his selection attractive to Herbert Walker and Holland Martin. Bulleid and Leonard Lynes soon designed 150 new carriages for the Bournemouth and Weymouth services, but unfortunately the outbreak of war prevented the order being completed. By 1938 rolling stock was appearing in the new bright 'malachite green' favoured both by Bulleid and the Chairman, Robert Holland Martin. The lettering 'Southern' on tenders and carriages also took a new form.

Even so, the Southern could not match the glamour of the LNER High Speed Trains or the LMS 'Coronation Scot'. The fastest run was Andover–Waterloo in 1939, at 58·6 mph – a long way behind what was being achieved elsewhere. Even the 'Atlantic Coast Express' with its first stop at Salisbury, only $83\frac{3}{4}$ miles from Waterloo, and another stop before Exeter, could scarcely compare with the GWR non-stop run to Plymouth with the 'Riviera'. And the decision (shared with the GWR) to retain four-a-side seating without arm-rests in third-class corridor compartments did not match the LMS and LNER's more generous treatment of their long-distance passengers in their best trains.

On the other hand, a good deal of renovation was taking place in interior fittings, and in 1938 the last gas-lit Southern coach was withdrawn from service. On the Isle of Wight the last non-bogie passenger carriages had been replaced by 1939 with elderly but still comfortable bogie stock, brought over from the mainland by the Southampton floating crane. Only a few vans were reminders of the old four- and six-wheeled stock that used to jolt around the Island.

A few curious survivals of old railway practice persisted. One was the 5.25 pm train from London Bridge to Redhill, Dorking, Guildford, and Reading, a reminder of South Eastern Railway days. It had a return working which reached London Bridge at 9.48 am, so any Reading commuter who desired to explore the Home Counties instead of travelling to Paddington in a fraction of the time, could do so, taking advantage of the 'alternative route' fare. Railway archaeologists would also note a starting signal at Esher on the platform for the Sandown Park race traffic; it was an old three-position wooden semaphore which fell inside a slot in the post to give the 'clear' indication, a survival of time-interval working in the early days.

Other survivals were the 'birdcage' train sets, with their elevated look-outs for the guard working, among other services,

97

on the Oxted line. This route was something of a maverick in Southern terms. It long lacked any regular-interval service; and the locomotives which drew its trains were a curious collection. Nevertheless, it saw some through workings to Eastbourne via the 'Cuckoo Line' (Tunbridge Wells to Hailsham).

A piece of railway antiquity well overdue for modernisation was the Waterloo & City line, generally known as the 'Drain'. It had been the second 'tube' to be built in London, after the City & South London but before the Central London, in 1898. Just fractionally over 1½ miles long, with only two stations, it had been operated very much on main line principles, with block cabins at Waterloo and the Bank and semaphore signals in the stations. It suffered from gradients as steep as 1 in 30 and curves of only five chains radius.

Rolling stock was quite American in appearance, with passenger entry and exit through end platforms, the gates being controlled by the guards. The car bodies had in fact been supplied from the USA but assembled at Eastleigh. Siemens of Stafford had supplied the electrical gear.

In 1937 it was decided to build new rolling stock with power doors – 12 motor and 16 trailer cars – and relay the track, welded into 315-foot lengths, simultaneously moving the conductor rail from the centre to the normal position outside the running rails. Modern signalling was to be installed at the same time.

It was intended to provide escalators at the Bank to replace the long sloping subway, rising 41 feet and over 300 feet long, which generations of City men had cursed as they shuffled slowly up it in the morning peak hour. With a 3-minute headway in the peak, the trains packed to their utmost capacity, the subway at times became choked to an extent that made it impossible to walk through in less than 10 or 12 minutes – twice as long as the train journey! The Chairman, Robert Holland Martin, who regularly used the 'Drain' between his City and Waterloo offices, referred feelingly to this in announcing the improvements at the 1938 Annual General Meeting.

Unfortunately, the powers needed for the escalator were delayed owing to problems connected with the subsoil, and this major improvement had to be deferred until after the war, when it took the form of a 'travolator', not an escalator. The new rolling stock was not brought into use in Szlumper's time; it only started to run in October 1940, at the height of the London air raids. Opportunity then was taken to rename the City station 'Bank'.

Looking back over the results of the whole electrification policy since 1923, the Board and the management could feel well satisfied with the results. Total passenger journeys on the Southern rose, year by year, from 236 million in 1923 to a pre-war peak of 379 million in 1937, the Coronation year. (There was a slight fall, reflecting the international crisis, to 371 million in 1938.) In 1926, Charing Cross had handled a daily average total of 13,446 passengers between 7 am and 10 am. By 1938 this figure had risen to 37,095. At London Bridge, similar counts had shown an increase from 49,001 in 1933 to 60,034 in 1938; at Waterloo, from 36,415 in 1933 to 47,051 in 1938. Yet only about £20·5 million had been spent on the whole electrification programme.

Despite the reward of increased passengers, the economic depression of the 1930s had taken its toll of the Southern's finances. In 1923 the receipts from railway working were £25·8 million, and expenses £19·3 million – an operating ratio (percentage of receipts absorbed by working expenses) of 74 per cent. At the bottom of the depression in 1932 the corresponding figures were £19·7 million and £16·0 million, representing a worsened operating ratio of 80 per cent. The fall in net receipts had a serious effect upon the dividend position. Dividends on the preferred ordinary stock fell from 5 per cent to 1 per cent, and on the deferred ordinary from 3½ per cent to nil in 1932. However, by 1938 the preferred divident had risen to 5 per cent once more, though there was still nothing paid on the deferred stock.

It must not be overlooked that other activities contributed to the results in good years. It was once said that the Southern was a docks and shipping enterprise that also ran a railway! The return on the lower-rated stocks largely depended on the state of international trade, both passenger and freight, as reflected in the net receipts from (1) docks, especially Southampton; (2) ships; and (3) Continental boat trains (with their enhanced fares).

This financial record may not seem brilliant, but it was the best of those of the four main lines. The Great Western only maintained a dividend on its ordinary stock by drawing on reserve funds. The Southern in fact weathered the depression very well, all things considered. Much of its passenger traffic, being short-distance, was exceptionally vulnerable to road competition, and only electrification had enabled the railway to fight back effectively.

The Southern's response to economic difficulties was not to cut back on services; on the contrary, not only did the public get good service from timetables that started not long after 5 am and often ended well after midnight; the operators extracted maximum utilisation from rolling stock that might be kept on the move, in some diagrams, for 18 or 19 hours out of the 24. On the commercial side, Missenden as Traffic Manager instituted a 'Southern Sales League'. Each station's performance and potential traffic were studied and target figures issued to it. Meritorious performance in relation to the target was marked by the presentation of inscribed silver shields or cups.

By 1938 the Railway Companies Association, representing the interests of the Boards and the shareholders, had decided to make urgent representations to the government about the need to relax the long-standing statutory controls over their charges for freight traffic, in order that the railways might compete with road haulage on more equitable terms. It was rather ironic that, whilst the Southern had by far the least interest in freight of all the main line companies, it fell to Robert Holland Martin to lead a deputation of the four Chairmen to meet the Minister of Transport, Leslie Burgin, on 23 November 1938. He was accompanied by Lord Stamp of the LMS, Lord Palmer of the GWR, and Sir Ronald Matthews of the LNER.

This official approach was backed up by a propaganda campaign for a 'Square Deal', with posters and publications presenting the railways' case. John Elliot was the Southern's representative on a Steering Committee of Assistant General Managers from the GWR and LNER, with a senior commercial man from the LMS, which planned the whole strategy. Eventually the Companies obtained from the government a promise to do something – a promise overtaken by the events of September 1939.

'Ancestral voices prophesying war' in fact formed a sombre counterpoint to the Southern Railway's more cheerful activities during Szlumper's General Managership. It was clear that if war with Germany came, the Southern would be in the forefront owing to its geographical position. The first emphasis was on the training of staff in air-raid precautions. In 1938 G. Wynne Davies was appointed ARP officer, and classes were soon held at centres in London and West Croydon, followed by Eastleigh, Ashford and New Cross. By 1939 an ARP instructional train had been fitted up and was touring the system.

After the Munich crisis of 1938 the pressure rapidly increased. Intensive bombing of London from the outset was expected, and the railways were encouraged by the government to find emergency centres outside the capital to ensure continuity of management. The Southern's wartime head-quarters was arranged in Deepdene House near Dorking, a former stately home that had been visited by Winston Churchill, and where Disraeli had written one of his novels. It had been built in the Regency style for Thomas Hope, a wealthy London connoisseur of art. After the First World War it had become a hotel and was somewhat run-down when the Southern bought it. It stood in extensive grounds, including an underground reservoir and caves. It was rumoured on the Southern that Bulleid, who lived nearby, had identified it as convenient and 'sold' the idea of purchase to the General Manager.

The caves were extensive enough to provide a control office, a telephone exchange and some bedrooms; the stable block accommodated forty bedrooms plus some offices; while the main building became an office block.

The evacuation plans provided for Deepdene to house the General Manager, Traffic Manager, Superintendent of Operations, Locomotive Running Superintendent, Chief Engineer and Accountant. Other emergency centres were set up at Woking for the London (West) Divisional Superintendent, Divisional Engineer and Divisional Locomotive Running Superintendent. Equivalent centres were created for the London (East) Division at Orpington, and at Redhill for the London (Central) Division.

Walker had always set his face against centralised operating

101

control offices of the type in use on the LMS and the LNER. But in anticipation of war conditions an extended telephone network was installed during 1938 and 1939 at a total cost of £130,000. The development of 'Control' on the Southern is described in Appendix 2.

Deepdene, incidentally, gave its name to a set of signalling and other regulations which were applied to special or ordinary trains conveying royalty and VIPs, other than the King and heads of state. The 'Deepdene' regulations were less restrictive than the full Royal Train regulations, which required, for example, double block working to be instituted and tunnels inspected. (The Royal Train regulations were coded 'Grove', derived from The Grove, the LMS wartime headquarters near Watford.)

As war preparations accelerated, a number of old Stroudley D class 0–4–2T engines were equipped with steam pumps for firefighting, water being taken from the tender of a locomotive alongside. The Southern also contributed to the stock of casualty evacuation trains, made up from bogie vans with stretchers, plus an open third for attendants, and brake vans at each end.

Until war actually broke out it was assumed that Szlumper, although a keen Territorial soldier with the rank of Colonel, would carry on at Waterloo. But almost immediately after hostilities started the War Office asked Holland Martin if Szlumper could be released to become Director-General of Transportation and Movements, largely because of his expert knowledge of Southampton, which was being used as the principal port of embarkation for the British Expeditionary Force. Holland Martin consulted colleagues on the Board and agreed, in his impulsive way, before consulting Szlumper, that Szlumper could be released and that Missenden would be acting General Manager in his absence.

The Chairman had miscalculated. Szlumper agreed to go, on the understanding that he would return after the war. But Missenden flatly refused to accept an acting appointment. He told Holland Martin that the choice was between the *status quo* and a substantive appointment as General Manager, or else he would resign. Missenden, in fact, knew well that he was almost indispensable, Szlumper having relied upon him heavily on the traffic side – and he forced the Board to offer a substantive appointment. Szlumper, perhaps unwisely, did not allow this to stop himself from going to the War Office, where he was later gazetted Major-General. His line of retreat had, however, been cut off: the Southern came under Missenden for nearly all its remaining existence.

Missenden was a very experienced, careful, competent railwayman, who had risen from the bottom of the ladder. His was not a warm personality; his lack of formal education made him distrustful, even resentful, of 'intellectuals'. He had a prejudice against politicians and civil servants. But he delegated well, keeping a sharp eye on the performance of subordinates. He refused to work long hours and he did not express himself well on paper, apart from standard railway departmental jargon. He possessed a tough moral if not physical fibre. Always realistic, he usually managed to keep the loyalty of those who served him well by ensuring that they were suitably rewarded. His sponsorship of Elliot – a personality as unlike his own as it is possible to imagine – is testimony to that. Elliot, promoted to Deputy General Manager, was invaluable to Missenden; a man of the world, with wide outside contacts, he complemented his chief's solid, if rather unimaginative, professional competence. Together they made a strong team for the tasks of wartime transport.

Chapter 11

THE SOUTHERN'S FREIGHT

Although three-quarters of its rail traffic receipts came from passengers, the Southern's freight had many interesting features, primarily determined by the character of the south and west of England, and the general absence of heavy industry. That meant that a very large proportion of freight transits were to and from 'foreign' lines. Coal and other fuels flowed in from South Wales, the Midlands and the North of England, together with manufactured articles of every description. Outwards moved the products of agriculture and light industry, though there were also some interesting bulk traffics. These included paper products and cement from the Medway area, gypsum from the mine at Mountfield, Kentish hops for breweries, and milk in large quantities from the dairying industries of Wiltshire, Dorset, Somerset and Devonshire. Even the Isle of Wight produced quite a substantial seasonal sugar beet traffic.

There were many private sidings for industries along the south bank of the Thames, some in the area of Woolwich Arsenal and originally stimulated by wartime demands. Coal came from the four Kent collieries near Dover – Tilmanstone, Betteshanger, Snowdown and Chislet. These pits supplied some of the locomotive coal requirements of the Southern – not always to the delight of firemen and Running Shed Superintendents. The Betteshanger coal was least popular; that from Chislet and Snowdown was more usually satisfactory. But enginemen really preferred the Welsh steam coal which the South Western section received via Salisbury. The Brighton and the South Eastern's coal, largely from the Midlands or Yorkshire, arrived through the London exchanges.

Turning to foodstuffs, fruit and vegetables from the Channel

Islands, and indeed from many countries overseas, helped to make Southampton's imports – especially of South African produce – very important. In the 1930s R. M. T. Richards was sent to South Africa to secure business for the Southern; he succeeded, in that through rates were offered for traffic consigned through to London by the Union Castle line and the Southern.

Generally, centres away from London did not have very large goods stations – nothing comparable with Birmingham's Lawley Street or Liverpool's Huskisson. London was the freight magnet, and here each of the pre-Grouping constituents had had quite substantial terminals – Nine Elms on the LSWR, Willow Walk for the LBSCR and the adjacent Bricklayer's Arms for the SECR. Bricklayer's Arms and Willow Walk were combined in March 1932, and were known thereafter officially by the former's title – to the staff, 'B.A.', or 'The Brick'.

Each terminal was fed from a marshalling yard that separated out the London-terminating traffic from the cross-London exchanges with other railways. Feltham was much the largest and most modern; it was also a partly mechanised hump yard, owing much to the enterprise of Sir Herbert Walker in his LSWR days, though it did not include wagon retarders. Norwood yard served the Brighton side, and Hither Green sidings the South Eastern. Near Loughborough Junction, the former LCDR line to Holborn Viaduct was equipped with Herne Hill Sorting Sidings, which dealt particularly with traffic for the north over the Widened Lines – of which more later. There was also a 'Grande Vitesse' depot for Continental traffic (which Americans would call express freight), largely handled by forwarding agents working for importers and exporters. This was situated at Blackfriars, just south of the Thames railway bridge; it was an ex-LCDR depot, largely used by wine importers. There was also an ex-South Eastern Grande Vitesse depot at Gravel Lane in Southwark – later named Ewer Street, eventually just Southwark, immediately on the Waterloo side of Metropolitan Junction, at the westernmost point of the Cannon Street triangle. 'Petite Vitesse', or ordinary Continental freight, was mainly handled through Newhaven.

In addition to its own freight depots, the Southern accommodated a number of 'foreign' railway depots, mainly for the coal traffic. LMS depots were at Walworth Road, Clapham Wharf, Knight's Hill, Brockley Lane, and Brixton; LNER depots were at Elephant & Castle, New Cross, and Brockley. They were awkward from an operating point of view and were usually served by trip workings by the 'foreign' company concerned. The Southern also owned a number of Thames-side wharves, at Battersea, Nine Elms, Charlton (Angerstein) and Deptford. They were used by barge traffic, mainly from London Docks. Nine Elms was equipped with a modern granary in the 1930s for warehousing on a large scale, with chutes and hoists for bagged traffic.

Mechanisation within depots was not adopted to any noticeable extent. But motor collection and delivery vehicles increased steadily from only 140 in 1923 to 736 in 1938, though an appreciable proportion of the collection and delivery work remained horsedrawn. In 1938 there were still 602 horses on the Southern's payroll, but Bricklayer's Arms collection and delivery work was generally modernised in the mid-1930s, with the introduction of the three-wheeled tractors known as 'mechanical horses', though some horse cartage continued well into the 1940s. Much parcels and 'sundries' work at smaller stations was contracted out to delivery agents who were established local carriers. This practice was slow to disappear, even after nationalisation, and probably reflected Walker's philosophy that non-railway tasks could well be left to outsiders.

The Southern exchanged traffic with the Great Western at Basingstoke, from which the main routes led via Reading and Oxford to Birmingham and the Black Country; and via Banbury, Woodford Halse and the former Great Central main line to the industrial Midlands. At Salisbury the Great Western led away to Bath, Bristol and South Wales, whilst there were subsidiary exchange points such as Templecombe for the Somerset & Dorset Joint Line, Andover for the Midland and South Western Joint, and of course the GWR/SR meeting points at Exeter and Plymouth.

Geographical reasons determined that the 'foreign' line exchanges of the ex-LBSCR and ex-SECR networks were in London, the one exception being Reading, where the curious penetrating arm of the former South Eastern Railway joined the Great Western to form a cross-country route of considerable strategic as well as freight significance; it was to play a key role in the rail movements after Dunkirk in 1940.

The London exchanges were effected by several routes. The North and South West Junction line was of key importance to ex-LSWR traffic since it directly connected Feltham yard via Hounslow, Old Kew Junction and Acton Wells Junction with the ex-Great Central line at Neasden and the ex-Midland line at Brent Junction. From Acton Wells Junction a connection led via Willesden Junction (High Level) to the North London line through Hampstead Heath, continuing from Gospel Oak over the Tottenham and Hampstead Joint Line (LNER and LMS) to the ex-Great Eastern at Tottenham (for the Cambridge main line) or into Temple Mills Marshalling Yard, with a further connection to the Tilbury and Southend section of the LMS at Barking. Workings from Feltham to the ex-Great Eastern Colchester line generally used the North London route via Dalston Junction, Victoria Park and Channelsea Junction, for Stratford.

Next in importance came the West London and West London Extension Railways (the former joint GWR/LMS and the second joint GWR/LMS/SR) linking Willesden Junction (for former LNWR routes) and North Pole Junction (for the GWR) with Clapham Junction for ex-LSWR and ex-LBSCR lines and Longhedge Junction for ex-SECR lines. The difficulties of the cross-London trip workings were greatly eased when in 1929 the Nunhead and Lewisham loops were opened, enabling traffic from the Widened Lines to reach Hither Green more easily than via London Bridge.

The North and South West Junction also carried passenger trains though much fewer than in earlier days. Only the North London electric service from Broad Street to Richmond traversed it from Acton Wells Junction to South Acton. The West London's passenger workings were more substantial and were centred on its principal station at Addison Road, Kensington (now renamed Olympia). The LMS provided quite a frequent electric service between Willesden Junction (High Level) and Earl's Court. And the Metropolitan Railway (later

London Transport) operated another electric service between Edgware Road and Addison Road. Between Addison Road and Clapham Junction the Southern maintained a steam passenger service to Clapham Junction, operating (in principle) alternately to the 'South Western' or the 'Brighton' sides of that station. Tradition died hard in that the former's trains were usually drawn by M7 0–4–4T ex-LSWR engines, the latter's by Stroudley D1 0–4–2Ts. In consequence of this frequent line occupation by passenger trains, the freight trains had to queue up and were in fact often worked through Addison Road station on 'permissive block', buffered up together on the centre through roads so that the passenger trains could overtake them by using the platform loops. A further complication to the freight workings was the 'Sunny South Expresses', originally introduced before the First World War (and then named 'Sunny South Specials'), connecting Liverpool and Manchester direct with Brighton, Eastbourne, Hastings and the Kent coast resorts. At various times other through portions had been carried and there were reliefs in the summer holiday season which could badly affect the West London's freight working.

If the NSWJ line was the chief cross-London artery on the South Western side, and the WLR on the Brighton side, the Widened Lines of the Inner Circle, built by the Metropolitan Railway, were largely used by the South Eastern side. This route left the Holborn Viaduct line South of that terminus and, via Snow Hill, joined the Moorgate–King's Cross Widened Lines just east of Farringdon. At King's Cross the ex-GNR main line was reached via the Hotel Curve – a steeply graded and sulphurous stretch of tunnel hated by engine crews – and at Kentish Town the Midland main line was joined.

The Widened Lines suffered from a number of disadvantages. The LMS and LNER passenger services to and from Moorgate, quite frequent in the morning and evening peaks, restricted the use by freight at such periods. The curves and steep if short gradients limited the number of wagons per train. The gradient in the southbound direction up to the Blackfriars railway bridge was so severe that trains had to be banked in the rear. For this purpose a tank engine known as the 'Snow Hill Banker' was permanently stationed on a short siding just West of Farringdon station, where it simmered peacefully away for long periods interrupted by short periods of hectic activity as far as the middle of the bridge, where it would reverse and drop back to its place of repose.

The last North–South route was the least satisfactory from an operating point of view. It was the East London Railway which linked New Cross and New Cross Gate (ex-SECR and ex-LBSCR respectively) with the former Great Eastern line at Shoreditch. Unfortunately, the connection was originally designed not for freight but for passenger services (long since abandoned) which ran to and from Liverpool Street main line terminus. Every freight train therefore had to enter the passenger station and reverse, so that such movements had to be virtually confined to the dead of night. There was also a wagon hoist at Spitalfields, giving a connection into Bishopsgate goods station, but as can be imagined its throughput could only be very limited; its capacity was two four-wheeled wagons at a time.

Added to these handicaps was the fact that the Metropolitan Line operated quite a frequent electric service from Hammersmith to, alternately, New Cross and New Cross Gate. So the East London's defects were not redeemed by its historic interest, traversing as it did Sir Marc Isambard Brunel's original Thames Tunnel.

To carry these varied traffics, the Southern started life with no less than 35,905 wagons. As one would expect, most were merchandise wagons, open and covered. Coal and other minerals were mainly carried in private owner's wagons, right up to the date of nationalisation. Braked stock was used for perishable traffic which moved at practically passenger train speeds, especially on the Continental services and those serving the port of Southampton. Some interesting Southern features included bogie brake vans, virtually unknown on other railways, specifically provided for the Nine Elms–West of England express goods trains, the fastest of which had a maximum permitted speed of 60 mph. Goods guards appreciated (and needed) their extra riding comfort. The vans were economically built by using the underframes of the motor luggage vans displaced by the conversion of the ex-LBSCR electric AC network, which were too short to be re-used for new carriages.

109

Another Southern speciality was a pioneer road-rail vehicle in the form of a flat wagon constructed to carry 2,000-gallon milk tanker road trailers. The trailers were hauled up a hinged ramp on to the rail wagon by means of a winch operated by the road tractor at the loading station. These wagons ran between Cole, Somerset, and Clapham Junction. Glass-lined milk tanks on rail underframes were used to bring milk to the large depot at Vauxhall, though the wagons were owned by United Dairies. The 40-ton bogie steel hopper wagons used for the Engineer's ballast trains from Meldon Quarry were also noteworthy, while insulated containers were in later years built for perishable traffic, especially meat imported through Southampton.

The Southern's freight trains fell into three main groups. First, of course, came the major services on the main lines, such as Southampton direct to Nine Elms, for instance with perishable import traffic, or the nightly Exmouth Junction to London fast goods with a wide range of wagons for various destinations. In 1947, for instance, the evening fast services from Nine Elms were: 7.25 pm (Southampton Docks); 9.10 pm (Plymouth Friary); 10.00 pm (Exmouth Junction); 10.38 pm (Weymouth); 11.22 pm (Southampton Docks); and 12.25 (Fratton). A nightly Exeter–Nine Elms fully-fitted freight was known variously as 'The Market', 'The Meat' or 'The Smithfield Flyer'. It stopped intermediately only at Templecombe and Salisbury.

One important feature of the Southern was that passenger train headways were so close in the electrified area that all freight moving during the daytime had to be briskly timed so as to avoid conflicting with the passenger service. One saw freight trains belting along at speeds that would startle, for instance, an LMS operator used to caravans of coal wagons crawling along the reserved 'goods lines' of the former Midland Railway. Many of these SR freight trains would be worked by pre-Grouping locomotives, since the Southern did not build new freight engines on any large scale. However, Maunsell did provide a freight version of the King Arthur class with smaller driving wheels (class S15) as well as a number of mixed traffic 2–6–0s. His last design, as it happens, was also a freight 0–6–0 of classic proportions, class Q.

Trip working was required at various places, including

110

Southampton Docks, Plymouth, the Kent coalfield and so on, but London was by far the most important. For such work, especially between Feltham and other London yards, Urie had provided some G16 4–8–0T engines mainly for hump shunting, and H16 4–6–2T machines for tripping. Maunsell followed with his 2–6–4T, class W, for trip working; his fondness for this wheel arrangement was not abated despite the 'River Cray' disaster.

The last category of freight, that over secondary and branch lines well away from the third rail, had considerable nostalgic charm since it was so completely different from the hustling Southern of the commuter business. A daily pick-up goods would pursue its leisurely way from station to station, shunting for maybe an hour or more at each. It could be headed by a wide variety of the elderly products of Adams, Drummond, Stroudley, R. Billinton, Kirtley or Wainwright. It was an epitome of the country railway, where on the 'Cuckoo Line' or the 'Bluebell and Primrose Line' (Tunbridge Wells–Hailsham and East Grinstead–Lewes, respectively) a goods train might make a 'stop in section' (*not* to be recorded in the guard's journal or the signalman's register) in order than a pheasant 'shot' with a well-aimed lump of coal could be collected and stored in the footplate tool-box. Another country custom in winter was a gesture from a signalman indicating that his supply of coal was running low, whereupon as the engine passed the fireman would obligingly throw out a few lumps of best locomotive coal to keep the kettle boiling on the signal-box stove. A chalk message on a board might serve the same purpose.

The Southern's major concern with passenger traffic was probably the reason why a 'Control' system as known on the other railways never appeared before the Second World War. The passenger business was expected to run to the timetable. If there was a delay leading to out-of-course running, action would normally be left to local management, mainly stationmasters and the 'reporting signalboxes', who were able to exercise discretion about diverting from through to local lines, or using a diversionary route. Nevertheless, especially on the freight side it was the practice to institute temporary controls for seasonal traffics – Kent soft fruit, for instance, and hop-pickers' specials being organised from telephone centres at Paddock Wood, Maidstone and Chatham. Special supervision was given to perishable traffic destined for markets, especially through the London termini. Supervisors' offices were installed in the principal London markets for this purpose. Nine Elms maintained a London Cartage Control, in addition to a Barge Control which covered the wharves and lighterage, as well as coastwise traffic at Deptford. These latter traffics experienced severe road competition in the later years of the Southern, though, as an offset, the rearmament programme eventually stimulated the use of private sidings in the dockyards of Portsmouth and Plymouth, as well as Woolwich Arsenal.

The complexity of the interaction between rail services, cartage, depot management and wharf traffic led to the creation of a post which departed from the standard Traffic organisation, namely that of a London District Freight Superintendent, to whom the yard managers were responsible, jointly with their responsibilities to the District Traffic Superintendent for purely operating matters.

With the outbreak of war and the institution of a Super-intendents' Committee of the Railway Executive Committee, it was inevitable that the Southern would be pressed to adopt a more continuous and centralised control system; the way and the extent to which this was implemented is set out in Appendix 2.

Finally, the Southern's freight, even though far from rivalling that of the other three groups, still amounted to a big business – 7·4 million tons of originating traffic in 1923, and, despite the growth of intense road competition meanwhile, remaining at 7·2 million tons in 1938. And the standard of service given to trade and industry, given some special problems of location and traffic volume, was clearly high. But was it all profitable? Even though so much was charged at the higher rates in the General Railway Classification for merchandise traffic, the costs of handling were inevitably high, especially having regard to the short length of haul for much of the business. Heavy bulk flows from the North, the Midlands and the Black Country had to be broken down with much trip and pick-up working. Small depots and wharves were costly to operate. So the Southern was probably right to consider its passenger business the key to its financial success; and in this it differed from the other groups, where freight was generally held to be more profitable than passenger traffic.

Chapter 12

THE SHIPPING SERVICES, THE CHANNEL TUNNEL, AND THE TRAIN FERRIES

From all its constituents the Southern inherited both shipping fleets and important continental traffic interests. On the SECR side, Folkestone was a railway-owned harbour, though Dover was an independent corporation. Newhaven was a railway-associated port on the LBSCR side; later under the Southern it became wholly owned. The Southampton Docks Company had been taken over by the LSWR in 1892, though there was also a Southampton Harbour Board which looked after the facilities not used by the railway. Each of these ports represented a major fleet base for railway steamers. Minor centres were at Portsmouth Harbour and Lymington Pier, both combining railway stations and terminals for Isle of Wight ferry services.

The railway fleets had been somewhat depleted during the First World War, but the Southern embarked on a substantial building programme very quickly. The 'house style' was also settled: buff yellow funnels with black tops, and a flag blue with a red St George's cross superimposed upon a white one, with the letters 'S.R.' in the first and fourth quarters. Only the Newhaven fleet did not conform. The fleet was jointly owned with the Etat Railway and so the ships continued to wear a joint house flag.

It would be tedious to catalogue every ship owned or built by the Southern, particularly as in the 1920s the proportion of cargo steamers was – to modern eyes – surprisingly high. Some must be named, however. The best ships inherited on the Dover-Folkestone station were the *Riviera* and the *Engadine*, built in 1911, the *Biarritz*, built in 1914, and the *Maid of Orleans*, built in 1918, all fine turbine steamers capable of 22–23 knots. There was also a fleet of cargo ships, bearing the names of towns on the SECR. The ex-Brighton Newhaven fleet was unlike that of Dover-Folkestone, where the English vessels sailed together with French ones owned by the Chemin de fer du Nord's associate company, SAGA (Société Anonyme de Gérance et d'Armement'. The LBSCR had had a 'treaty' with the Chemin de fer de l'État under which the ships of the Newhaven–Dieppe route were all jointly owned, though the registration and the actual ensigns under which they sailed had of course to be national. The *Brighton* and the *Dieppe* were the older ships (1903) supplemented by the more modern *Paris* and *Versailles* of 1921, with speeds of 25 knots. (The higher speed on this route was required in view of the longer distance.) Here again there was a substantial subsidiary fleet of cargo vessels.

From the LSWR came the *Normannia* and the *Hantonia* of 1911 for the Southampton–Havre route, and the *Princess Ena* for the St Malo service. The Channel Islands route was mainly in the hands of the *Vera, Alberta* and *Lorina*. The *Lorina* (of 1918) was named after Sir Herbert Walker's second wife. There was also, of course, a supporting fleet of smaller ships and cargo vessels. There was no French participation in the Southampton-based services.

The energy with which the Southern started replacing both older ships and losses during the 1914–1918 war is shown by the following total building achieved during its first ten years:

SOUTHERN RAILWAY SHIPS BUILT

	Car Ferry (incl. Isle of Wight)	Passenger	Cargo	Total
1924	—	3	2	5
1925	—	2	5	7
1926	—	—	2	2
1927	1	1	—	2
1928	1	3	1	5
1929	—	1	—	1
1930	1	4	—	5
1931	1	—	—	1
1932	—	1	—	1
Totals	4	15	10	29

115

After a decade, the Dover-Folkestone station had 9 passenger and 7 cargo ships; Newhaven had 7 passenger and 4 cargo vessels; and Southampton boasted 11 passenger and 6 cargo vessels. The Isle of Wight ferries accounted for 12 smaller ships – a total SR fleet of no less than 56 vessels.

A few noteworthy ships built by the Southern must be mentioned. In 1925 a fine pair – the *Isle of Thanet* and the *Maid of Kent* 21-knot vessels – were commissioned for the Dover–Calais and Folkestone–Boulogne routes respectively. In 1928 came the *Worthing* for Newhaven–Dieppe, with a speed of 25 knots, and a new *Brighton* in 1933. But perhaps the most famous of all vessels on the Southern, the much-loved *Canterbury* (2,909 gross tons), appeared in 1929. Her graceful lines and her speed ($25\frac{1}{2}$ knots) marked her out as the flagship which she undoubtedly was, being designed for the prestigious first-class 'Golden Arrow' London–Paris Pullman service. She had a passenger certificate for over 1,000 but was intended to carry only 300 VIP train passengers, for whom customs and immigration facilities were 'streamlined' both at Dover and Calais. *Canterbury* had a shelter deck with large plate-glass windows and armchairs for her pampered Pullman passengers. Her amenities included a 'Palm Court' and a buffet as well as a dining saloon. The Pullman car conductors for a time travelled through to Paris, returning the following day; on the ship they made reservations for passengers and on the trains ensured everyone's comfort.

Before very long the changing international financial situation made it necessary for *Canterbury* to accommodate ordinary train passengers as well as those in the 'Arrow', though maintaining special reserved seating for the Pullman patrons. It had proved uneconomic to operate this splendid ship for such small numbers of passengers.

Canterbury was followed by two new ships for the Channel Islands service, and then by the first car ferry – a portent of things to come – the *Autocarrier* of 1931. A relatively modest start was made with this vessel of only 822 gross tons, with a capacity for 35 cars. Its crossing time was $1\frac{3}{4}$ hours from Dover to Calais; loading and off-loading were time-consuming, being performed by cranage. It was, however, necessary to combat the

116

37　The 'Sunny South' near St Quintin Park on the West London line (note conductor rails, for the Willesden–Earl's Court service)

38　Closure of the Dyke branch – the last 'push-pull' leaving Devil's Dyke on 31 December 1938

39   Leaving Feltham Yard – a freight, hauled by 'H16' 4-6-2T

40   Cross-London trip working: climbing up from Snow Hill (note LCDR type signal)

41 Typical pick-up branch goods train – 9.42 am Farnham to Bordon

42 A 'foreign' depot on the S.R. – the LMS coal sidings at Walworth

43   PS 'Sandown' leaving Ryde Pier Head for Portsmouth in 1938

44   The pioneer car-carrier – S.S. 'Autocarrier'

45   The glamour of the 'Night Ferry': waiting to leave Victoria in 1936

46   Wagons being shunted on to the ferry at Dover

47 The ships on the Newhaven–Dieppe service were marginally faster than those on the Dover station as a rule, partly on account of the longer sea distance. S.S. 'Brighton'

48 Aerial view, showing the huge reclamation area of the new dockland

49 (above) S.S. 'Homeric' at Southampton in 1936

50 (left) A red-letter day for Southampton

51 (below) An ex-Brighton 'Terrier' 'AIX' on a
Newport–Freshwater train

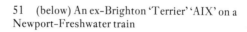

52   Shunting at Ventnor; a Beyer Peacock–built 2-4-0T 'Bonchurch' in 1927

53   Push-pull unit at Ventnor West (ex-I.W.C.R.)

competition offered by Townsend Bros, who had entered this field in 1930 with a converted minesweeper, the *Forde*, which could carry 30 cars. Townsends had previously been in the coastwise trade, and had entered the Dover–Calais route for cargo work in 1928. The Southern Railway would have then done well to buy them out – which would have been quite possible – had the huge expansion in roll-on, roll-off after the Second World War been foreseen.

On the freight side, the Southern ships had to face competition from other operators in the short-sea routes. But in the passenger field, in conjunction with their French partners, they maintained a dominant position across the Channel, apart from the monopoly of the Ostend trade exercised by the state-owned Belgian Marine.

The last ship ordered before the war by the Southern was a new *Invicta* (carrying on a traditional LCDR name), intended to replace the *Canterbury* as the flagship on the Dover station. She was to become very well known, though she was only commissioned in 1940 and immediately went on war service. A fine ship, her lines nevertheless lacked the extreme grace of the *Canterbury*, though having the advantage of an additional deck. But she took over the 'Golden Arrow' service soon after it was restored after the war. *Invicta* and her master, Captain Payne, Commodore-Master of the Dover-Folkestone fleet, became almost the symbol of Southern shipping.

He was in fact something of a national figure. He had been invited to take the salute from the royal box at the Royal Tournament and will long be remembered for the short speech he made when Master of the *Maid of Orleans* to his officers and ratings immediately before his ship was to take part in the D-Day operation. His words were taken down by the ship's radio officer and are repeated here by permission of his widow.

Well, lads, I am not telling you what to do because I know you will do it. The time has come when we are called upon to help in the great effort of liberating Europe, and you men of the Merchant Service do not require a lot of detailed instructions. Given the bare outline of a job, you do it without the blare of trumpets, but by sheer indomitable guts, exactly the same as

117

those old-timers who beat the sailing ships round the Horn. The Empire is watching and will be proud of you; the Company will be proud of you, and I am sure will remember each one of you as their men who sailed in one of their ships on that glorious day. I know you all personally, and I promise that in the days to come I will do my utmost to help you and remind the authorities that you were of the gallant group who sailed on that eventful evening with a light heart and firm resolve.

By doing your duty quietly you will be helping me and by so doing helping each other. Our job is to deliver the troops and keep on delivering. My job is triple, the safe conduct of the troops and you, but that doesn't worry me, because I know you will help me. An appropriate omen – Joan of Arc, Maid of Orleans, liberated France; this 'Maid' will help to do so again by the grace of God. Do not think I am any braver than you because I am not. I would much rather be in my garden at peace or in a pub, but this job has got to be done or you and yours would become worse than slaves. And when this show is over you will be able to walk with dignity among your friends both in Britain and France. Good luck to you all.

The Southern was not just a railway-owned shipping line that would be caught up in any European war involving Britain; it had long and close links with France that gave it international importance. Just as Captain Payne was a symbol of Southern shipping in the narrow seas, Arthur Newbold, General Agent for France, was for a long time a very significant figure in Anglo-French trade circles, being President of the British Chamber of Commerce in France. Some British railwaymen were surprised when he received a CBE, until they learnt that this was in the Foreign Office list, on the recommendation of HM Ambassador in Paris.

Turning to operations nearer home, the Southern did not neglect the Isle of Wight services, and put some fine paddle steamers on the Portsmouth–Ryde run. It may have seemed late in the day to adhere to paddlers, but their manoeuvrability in confined areas was a continuing advantage. And, for the road vehicle traffic, a car ferry with roll-on, roll-off facility was built to operate between Portsmouth and Fishbourne, followed by a Lymington–Yarmouth car ferry in 1938.

One serious competitor was of course the airline industry, growing fast after a hesitant start in about 1919; it is considered in Chapter 15. A possible threat to the shipping services, though not to the railway's continental business, was the proposal to build a Channel Tunnel which took shape in the later 1920s, reviving Sir Edward Watkin's frustrated project of the 1880s. When the Board of Trade, at the pressing of the War Office, ordered the cessation of work on Watkin's Tunnel, a small but unforeseen bonus for the railway emerged. Trial borings had revealed that under the Lower Chalk through which the tunnel was to be excavated there was a workable seam of coal of fair quality. Eventually four collieries (Tilmanstone, Chislet, Snowdown and Betteshanger) were established in Kent, not under the Shakespeare Cliff where the Tunnel borings were started but inland; they produced both locomotive and steamship coal for the Southern and also some welcome traffic on rail.

Returning to the Tunnel, the development of electric traction had made this a much more practicable proposition than when Watkin had optimistically offered to run steam trains under the Channel. Discussions between the Southern Railway and the Chemin de fer du Nord (which had long been backed by the Rothschilds) resulted in a firm proposal, for which the railways were prepared to find the money. The British Government of the day issued a White Paper which discussed the project in an inconclusive way. Matters were brought to a head on 30 June 1930 when a Resolution affirming parliamentary support for a Tunnel was moved by Mr E. Thurtle, a Labour member, and seconded by Sir B. Peto, a Conservative. The speeches on both sides of the House of Commons were virtually confined to exposing prejudices and preconceived ideas; there was no real discussion of the economic issues or the financial prospects. Opponents included Sir Samuel Hoare (later the signatory of the infamous Hoare-Laval pact), who voiced the sort of military objections that had been put forward in 1882, and – surprisingly – Herbert Morrison, the Labour Party transport spokesman. Support came largely from Labour back-benchers. The Prime Minister, J. Ramsay MacDonald, made a lengthy speech which can only be described as woolly, indicating that on balance he felt too many doubts and saw too many difficulties to support the Tunnel.

On a free vote, the results were:

For the Resolution	172
Against	179
Majority against	7

This obviously put paid to the Tunnel for the foreseeable future, since parliamentary approval was needed for the legal and legislative formalities involved, including a treaty with France.

The Southern was not put off in its search for better Continental connections and Walker began to consider a train ferry service. Such had in fact been proposed as long ago as 1868, but Admiralty objections (very hard to understand) had silenced the arguments in favour. Even so, train ferries had quite a respectable ancestry. The first had been started across the Firth of Forth in 1850, followed by one across the Firth of Tay in 1851. Valuable experience had been gained during the 1914–18 War when Richborough had been developed as a temporary but still quite effective ferry terminal, handling large quantities of rolling stock. But Richborough was unsuitable as a permanent peacetime terminal, partly on account of its need for constant and costly dredging.

The Southern, in conjunction with the Nord Railway, promoted the construction of a ferry dock with entrance locks at Dover, and a link-span in the existing enclosed basin at Dunkirk. The ships acquired were three, named *Twickenham Ferry, Hampton Ferry* and *Shepperton Ferry*. The first-named sailed under the French flag. All three had a speed of 16½ knots, a passenger certificate of 500, and tonnages between 2,839 gross tons (*Twickenham Ferry*) and 2,996 tons (*Shepperton Ferry*). All came from Swan Hunter and Wigham Richardson of Wallsend, whereas normally Southern ships were built by Denny Bros of Dumbarton.

In addition to extensive train-ferry wagon services, a nightly through sleeping car train between London and Paris was introduced. The sleeping cars were provided by the Wagons-Lits Company and of course had to conform to the more restricted British loading gauge and to Continental standards of brakes, buffing gear and couplings. Originally eleven cars were built for the service; five more were constructed in 1939, but stored until after the war.

A full account of Britain's only international train has been given by George Behrend and Gary Buchanan in *Night Ferry*. Romantic it certainly was when seen at night at Victoria Station, in the blue livery of the Compagnie Internationale des Wagons-Lits et des Grands Express Européens. As a practical substitute for the Channel tunnel, it had many shortcomings. The journey time of nearly 11 hours was excessive; trans-shipment was accompanied by loud clanking of chains in the middle of the night; rough weather in the Channel could be very unpleasant; and punctual arrivals were the exception rather than the rule – at any rate, until John Elliot took a personal interest in improving standards in this respect, an improvement not destined to survive long after nationalisation. Even so, the Night Ferry had its many devotees, including after 1936 the Duke of Windsor. It was an imaginative concept, bringing a touch of glamour to the suburban stations it travelled through in the morning light on its way to, usually, a late arrival at Victoria.

Chapter 13

THE SOUTHAMPTON STORY

Southampton is an historic port with great natural advantages. First of course is the well-known feature of its two high tides, following each other from different sides of the Isle of Wight with a gap between them of only about two hours, so that there is a long period of high water. Then, the approach up Southampton Water, about six miles long and averaging about a mile across, is not merely completely sheltered but tends to be kept clear from silting by the scour of the two rivers which enter it just below the town of Southampton, the Test and the Itchen – two names sacred to fly-fishermen.

The triangular area between the two rivers has a long history, starting with the medieval building of wharves and roughly enclosed docks. But despite its natural advantages Southampton as a commercial port had a rather chequered history. The Hampshire coast is a long way from Britain's major industrial centres and Southampton could not match Liverpool's geographical advantage in relation to the industries of Lancashire and Yorkshire. Even London is quite distant, which may have induced the P&O Line to move its terminal to the Thames in 1882. Nevertheless, the nineteenth century saw energetic and successful development of the port. It really began with the construction in 1831 of the Town Quay and the Royal Pier, followed by the coming of the railway and the formation of the Southampton Dock Company, which built the Outer Dock and the Inner Dock. Southampton then developed both as a railway packet port and as a deep-sea liner port. The London & South Western began operating shipping services as early as 1845 to Le Havre, St Malo and the Channel Islands. Troopships for the Crimea sailed from here, the forerunners of many others, in other wars.

In the 1880s the Dock Company began to require much larger docks to accommodate the bigger liners then being built, but it only managed to construct the Empress Dock, opened in 1890, with a loan from the LSWR of £250,000. In 1892 the railway bought up the Dock Company and rapid expansion followed, including the building of a graving dock, new river quays and the Trafalgar Dock, opened in 1905 and enlarged, specifically to accommodate the White Star liner *Olympic*. A further dock opened in 1911 was called the Ocean Dock. The list of shipping companies using Southampton by then included many of the world's most famous names – White Star, Cunard, Royal Mail Steam Packet and Union Castle, to mention a few.

The railway steamers to France and the Channel Islands continued to use the Inner and Outer Docks, well served by a rail connection passing the Terminus Station and the dock gates – the Outer Dock for vessels in service, the Inner Dock for laid-up ships, the railway marine workshops being adjacent.

In LSWR days Walker had been deeply interested in Southampton's potential; not long after he took office at Waterloo the port's capacity was well shown by its use for the dispatch of the British Expeditionary Force to France in 1914. After the Southern Railway became responsible for the port, its first Docks and Marine Manager was G. S. Szlumper, son of the SR Chief Engineer, who had not merely held the Southampton post on the LSWR but had been closely associated with Walker as his Assistant at Waterloo and then as Secretary of the wartime Railway Executive Committee. His energetic temperament guaranteed that opportunities for development would not be overlooked. A new floating dock, in its day the largest in the world, able to accommodate vessels of 60,000 tons, was built on the Tyne and towed to Southampton in 1924. The voyage, achieved with seven tugs, took four days. The Prince of Wales officially opened the dock on 27 April 1924.

Looking further ahead, it was clear that the traditional port area had little room for expansion, being hemmed in by the built-up area and the two rivers. But to the west there stretched two miles of mudflats on the north side of the Test estuary,

123

ending in a spit of land at a place called Millbrook. The main line to Bournemouth ran parallel to this shore. At the east end was the suburb of Southampton named Blechynden and the station called Southampton West which, since the extension of the main line to Bournemouth, had really become the city's principal station.

The plan evolved was a bold one – to enclose 407 acres of mud flats by constructing a quay wall and infilling so as to reclaim the whole area to solid ground. Parallel with the quay wall a jetty 4,500 feet long would be built, 600 feet away from the quay. The chief architect of the great plan was the SR Docks Engineer, Wentworth-Shields.

Szlumper did not stay to see the project realised. He had been appointed in 1925 to the additional post of Assistant General Manager and in 1927 was called to Waterloo on a full-time basis. His successor at Southampton was his former Deputy, G. R. Newcombe, later followed by two important Southern figures, E. J. Missenden and R. P. Biddle.

Work started on the quay wall in February 1929, with pile-driving effected from timber staging. The fill for the reclaimed area came from the great Micheldever chalk pit between Winchester and Basingstoke and from the deepening of the channels to the berths. As the ground consolidated, railway lines were laid and then transit sheds and cranes were erected. The end-result was 3,500 feet of berthing space with a depth of 45 feet of water at low tide, and as much again with a guaranteed depth of 40 feet. Eight transit sheds were constructed and a new rail marshalling yard, connected with the existing dock lines at the east and west ends. The cost of the whole work was about £13 million.

The final touch was the construction of a new graving dock for the overhaul of the largest liners, upon which work started in 1931. This huge enclosed dock with its pumping machinery could accommodate ships of 100,000 tons. It was 1,200 feet long by 135 feet wide, and 45 feet deep. To withstand the weights involved the floor was of concrete 25 feet thick. The Graving Dock was eventually opened by King George V, who sailed in, accompanied by Queen Mary, in the Royal Yacht *Victoria and Albert* to perform the ceremony on 26 July 1933. The opening was marked by a crisis; the special train from Waterloo was ready to depart with distinguished invited guests when a message was received that the main line was blocked by an accident. Walker and Cox quickly decided: 'We will go over the Alps [that is, via Alton]. Send a message to keep the Royal Yacht out until we arrive.' Slow steaming up Southampton Water saved the day!

A major element in the Southern's planning was the attraction of industry to the new dockland area. An early success was scored when Messrs Rank erected the huge Solent Flour Mills for the milling of imported grain in the dock estate. This contributed to the westward drift of population and business activity in Southampton away from the historic city centre, and it was decided that the West station must be improved. It had originally been named Blechynden when first opened in 1850, but renamed Southampton West End when the tunnel spur from the original main line was opened a few years later. In 1895 it had been remodelled with some quite substantial brick buildings, including a clock tower, and renamed Southampton West.

Following the completion of the main part of the new docks, in 1934–5 the station was enlarged, the down platform being converted to an island and a new down platform built beyond it, with a bay, providing four through roads. The new down-side platform had buildings in contemporary style, sometimes unkindly described as 'Southern Odeon', but the up platform, with the main street entrance, retained many of the former buildings, including the clock tower, with some enlargement and face-lifting. Other improvements included replacing the nearby level crossing by a concrete bridge, and renaming the station Southampton Central. The four-tracking through the station was continued as far as Millbrook; new signal boxes were built at Central and Millbrook.

Despite all these improvements, the arrangements for handling ocean liner passengers and their luggage were felt to fall short of the ideal. Plans were therefore prepared for a new ocean terminal at the east end of the new docks, providing spacious waiting rooms, refreshment facilities, customs and immigration examination halls, and rail platforms under cover within the terminal. The architectural treatment was to be thoroughly modern and the general concept was intended to rival and indeed surpass any airline terminal at that date.

War conditions deferred the execution of this plan, but work was started by the Southern Railway after the end of hostilities. It was a rather bitter blow to Southern pride that when the new terminal was opened Southampton was in the process of being transferred to the nationalised Docks and Inland Waterways Executive. However, the Ocean Terminal was opened with due ceremony by the then Prime Minister, C. R. Attlee, on 31 July 1950, and it was a slight comfort that the new owners had confirmed the Southern's manager, 'Reg' Biddle, as the man in charge. As a postscript, it must be added that it was even sadder that the Ocean Terminal was built only a few years before the jet airliner began to kill ocean liner traffic. For a time, however, the Southern Region of British Railways continued to run boat-train specials from Waterloo, and some all-Pullman trains for first-class liner passengers. As long ago as 1931 the Pullman Car Company had invested in thirteen new cars specially for the Ocean Liner Expresses. Many famous people from all walks of life – politics, stage, screen and business – passed through the terminal in its short heyday in the 1950s.

Southampton's handover to the Docks and Inland Waterways Executive, and its subsequent transformation – and labour troubles – during the container revolution are outside the scope of this book. But Southampton was an outstanding example of how well railway and port operations could be integrated; it was inconsistent that the nationalised British Transport Commission, with a statutory duty to 'integrate', insisted upon breaking up the close interworking that had grown up under LSWR and Southern Railway auspices. Southampton was unique among railway ports in the facilities it offered for road traffic, which developed under the DIWE very strongly, even though Biddle – a thorough railwayman and the son of the former LSWR agent in Jersey – continued for a time to be responsible to the Southern management as Marine Manager. Biddle was excellent at human and industrial relations and received a knighthood later on, mainly due to recommendations from Southampton civic and business interests. It is also very fitting that the main highway through the docks area is named 'Herbert Walker Avenue'.

Chapter 14

AN ISLAND INTERLUDE

Until about the middle of the nineteenth century, the Isle of Wight must have been one of the most beautiful and unspoilt rural areas it is possible to imagine. Certainly it so struck the young Queen Victoria when she and her husband decided to make it a holiday home by building Osborne House near Cowes. Downland, cliffs, beaches and wooded valleys were still undamaged by the demands of the mass tourist trade. Pleasant Regency houses in the seaside towns and picturesque villages full of thatched roofs adorned rather than damaged the landscape, before the speculative builder got to work.

But the growth of holiday traffic from the mainland, stimulated by the increase in steamship ferry services, led to a demand for better internal transport in the island in the 1850s. Cowes, at the mouth of the River Medina, was then the chief port of entry. Ryde, with its enormous stretch of muddy foreshore at low tide and no natural harbour, was only later to develop its situation opposite to Portsmouth Harbour as the main gateway for tourists. So the first railway was opened between Cowes and the island's capital, Newport, in 1862. The distance was no more than $4\frac{1}{4}$ miles. But within two years a more important line was promoted to run from Ryde (St John's Road) to Shanklin. The objective was to link Ryde with the rapidly developing seaside resorts along the east and south coasts – Sandown, Shanklin and Ventnor. Named the Isle of Wight Railway, it was incorporated in 1860, reached Shanklin in 1864 and extended its line to Ventnor in 1866. It was the only railway in the island to become even moderately prosperous.

The Isle of Wight Railway terminated at St John's Road on the east side of Ryde, far from the pier which provided the only shipping connection. The Pier Company, however, operated a horse tramway as far as St John's Road from the pierhead. Both the London & South Western and London Brighton & South Coast Railways, which ran into Portsmouth, found this very unsatisfactory and they jointly formed the Ryde Pier & Railway Company to build a pier capable of handling ships at all states of the tide, with a railway station at its extremity and a line thence to Ryde Esplanade and, through a short tunnel, linking with the Isle of Wight Railway at St John's Road. This link opened in 1880; it was always operated by the IWR.

The latter was fortunate in that Captain Mark Huish, the formidable and very experienced General Manager of the London & North Western Railway, had retired to Bonchurch, just outside Ventnor, shortly before the IWR Company received its Act of incorporation. Huish was persuaded to join the Board in November 1861, after having already acted as a consultant, and was extremely helpful to this small railway in controlling construction costs and later arranging running powers for IWR trains over the Ryde Pier and Railway Company's line to the steamer pierhead.

Other lines were promoted to join the Cowes & Newport Railway, one from Ryde to Newport (1875), another from Sandown, opened in 1880, and in 1897 one from Newport to Godshill and St Lawrence, extended to Ventnor West in 1900, worked by the Isle of Wight Central Railway. The IWR had meanwhile opened a branch from Brading to Bembridge in 1882.

The least successful island railway was the Freshwater Yarmouth & Newport, opened in 1889 – built very cheaply with its stations at Yarmouth and Freshwater well away from the traffic centres of these towns. It was worked by the Isle of Wight Central from its opening in 1889 until 1913, when it decided to operate the service itself. This was an exciting time for the islanders, since a scheme for a railway tunnel to the mainland, originally promoted in 1901, was now being more actively pursued by the financier Sir Blundell Maple of the great furniture firm and builder of the Great Central Hotel, his friend Sir Sam Fay, General Manager of the Great Central Railway, and a local businessman, Frank ('Bulldog') Aman, of Totland Bay. In 1913 a private Act of Parliament was promoted for a railway leaving the Freshwater Yarmouth & Newport at a point between Yarmouth and Freshwater, passing in tunnel under the Solent and emerging to join the Lymington branch of the LSWR on the main branch. A triangular junction would have provided direct running from the mainland to Freshwater by one arm and to Yarmouth (for Newport and Ryde) by the other.

In the same year, the Freshwater Yarmouth & Newport had become extremely dissatisfied with the way in which its traffic was handled by the IWCR and it terminated its agreement with the larger company. An interesting development followed, in which Sir Sam Fay, a Hampshire man by birth, played an important part. He had started his railway career on the London & South Western before leaving to be General Manager of the Midland & South Western Junction Railway, a struggling concern which he greatly improved. He had returned to the LSWR as Superintendent of the Line in 1899, becoming General Manager of the Great Central in 1902. He therefore knew a great deal about the Isle of Wight's traffic potential.

The dispute between the Freshwater Yarmouth & Newport and the IWCR resulted in the former being evicted from the latter's Newport station and deprived of locomotives and rolling stock. Fay came to the rescue. First of all, an independent station (little more than a platform with a corrugated-iron shelter) was built at Newport. Then two locomotives were quickly provided, both 0–6–0 tank engines, one a saddle-tank and the other a second-hand Terrier from the LBSCR. No. 1 was painted in mid-green by the FYN (and later repainted in SR green as No. W1, and named 'Medina' in 1928). No. 2 was in LSWR colours, as that railway had bought it from the LBSCR for working the Lee-on-Solent branch. It was later named 'Freshwater'.

In addition there was a set of six four-wheeled carriages hastily supplied by the Great Central, also well appointed and resplendent in new paintwork. An oddity on the FYN at one period – as late as 1922 – was a petrol-driven railcar seating only twelve passengers for use as a 'boat train' connection, running non-stop between Yarmouth and Newport.

Sadly, these exciting prospects faded away. Sir Blundell Maple died and the outbreak of war in 1914 killed any prospect of pursuing the tunnel scheme, although the FYN (as related in

Chapter 1) argued (to no effect) in 1922 and 1923 that the possibility of a tunnel revival must enhance the value of the little railway in an amalgamation scheme.

The Southern Railway thus acquired in 1923 three Island railways. The IWR was just profitable, though all its profits were earned during the short summer season, chiefly from traffic to and from the mainland. The next, the Central, was a more shaky concern, though it derived some strength from its connection at Cowes with the Red Funnel steamer service from Southampton and, at the Medina Wharf, with the freight brought in by sea. Finally, the FYN line was never a viable proposition, especially once bus services began to operate. It had long been in receivership.

The Southern Railway's acquisitions thus covered 55¼ miles of route, almost all single-track, in addition to the short double-line Ryde Pier Head–St John's stretch. There were 18 locomotives, 122 passenger vehicles and 574 freight wagons.

The traffic prospects might be roughly reflected in the density of population per mile – 2,941 on the ex-IWR lines; 1,837 on the ex-IWCR lines; but only 1,341 (and that mostly at the Newport end) of the ex-FYN line.

The locomotives acquired by the Southern were:

From the Isle of Wight Railway
7 2–4–0T engines, built by Beyer Peacock between 1864 and 1883;

From the Isle of Wight Central Railway
4 similar 2–4–0T engines from Beyer Peacock, built between 1876 and 1898,
1 4–4–0T built by Black, Hawthorn & Co. in 1890,
4 Brighton-built 0–6–0T engines, built between 1872 and 1880;

From the Freshwater Yarmouth & Newport Railway
1 0–6–0ST built 1902, from the GCR,*
1 0–6–0T Terrier from the LBSCR – both engines purchased in 1913.

---

* Originally a contractor's locomotive, built by Manning Wardle.

The island locomotives were to be distinguished until 1932 by the initial 'W' before their numbers. All, following past IWR practice, were given names of places on the island – this rather unadventurous naming policy following that which Stroudley had employed on the LBSCR. For obvious reasons, no island locomotive ever sported the name 'Parkhurst'! Some engines imported, incidentally, had to be equipped with the Westinghouse brake, standard on the island.

The antique 2–4–0T 'Ryde' (mentioned in Chapter 4) continued to run until 1932 when it was 68 years old. It was then preserved for a time in Eastleigh works, but was scrapped in 1940, no doubt owing to the wartime drive for scrap supplies.

Inhabitants of the island had long been critical of their railways on account of high fares, often varied at short notice, and dilapidated passenger carriages. Practically all the stock had been acquired second-hand from mainland railways and four-wheelers predominated, one striking exception being an ex-Midland Railway twelve-wheeled clerestory vehicle used for push-pull working by the Isle of Wight Central. The Southern put it on four-wheeled bogies and removed the clerestory. The Southern continued the practice of 'cascading' old stock from the mainland – first with ex-LCDR six-wheelers altered to four-wheelers in close-coupled sets, then some bogie stock (three ex-LSWR sets), and later still some ex-SECR sets with the guard's 'birdcage' removed. SR 'utility vans' also appeared. Virtually the whole of the island railways' wagons (574 in 1923) were replaced by standard 12-ton open wagons.

Sir Herbert Walker arranged a Directors' visit to the island in August 1923, which gave the Board an insight into the problems and possibilities. It paved the way for the purchase of Ryde Pier as from 1 January 1924, with its little tramway. Walker revisited the island in December 1924 and then promised local interests that rail services would be improved. Walker's visit was to be followed by quite a number of such trips by chief officers of the Southern, who found that a day on the island could combine business with relaxation. A good start with improvements was made by sending over four 02 class ex-LSWR Adams 0–4–4T locomotives, which were eventually followed, once this class had been found highly suitable for this class of work, by no less than 17 more during the Southern's existence before nationalisation. Four Stroudley ex-LBSCR E1 0–6–0T engines were added to the stock in 1932 and 1933, and five AIY Terriers between 1927 and 1930. Some standardisation of motive power was thus achieved as the older engines were scrapped or sent to the mainland. A few ancients survived, however, notably 2–4–0T 'Ryde'.

The Southern soon began to demonstrate that it really meant to improve services. 'Assistant for the Isle of Wight' was an interesting post. Originally covering running and maintenance of engines and rolling stock, other responsibilities were added which made it virtually a miniature general managership.

The position was usually held by a young man expected to rise a long way in the main organisation, as was indeed the case. But it was also an enjoyable interlude in their careers, as senior railwaymen such as A. B. MacLeod (who held this position with distinction during the key period of improvements) and G. L. Nicholson have testified. Work in the island, moreover, must have been healthy; shortly before the Southern takeover there retired from the position of stationmaster at Brading, at the age of eighty-two, W. Wheway, who had been the guard of the very first train into Shanklin in 1864 and similarly into Ventnor in 1866! This feat of longevity was recorded in the *Southern Railway Magazine*, which introduced a regular feature of 'Island Jottings', starting in 1925.

Structural improvements included new work at Sandown and Shanklin stations in 1925, and the single track between Brading and Sandown was doubled in 1927. A signal-box and crossovers were installed at Smallbrook Junction, South of St John's Road, where the Newport and Ventnor lines diverged. Previously the junction had been at the station and the two tracks as far as Smallbrook were worked as independent single lines. That practice continued during the winter timetable but in the summer the box was switched in and a new double-line section between St John's Road and Smallbrook increased the line capacity, which was often stretched to the limit during August Saturdays.

Rather surprisingly, the Ryde pier tramway was converted in 1927 from electric traction to Drewry petrol railcars.

Along with better facilities, locomotives and rolling stock, services and speeds improved. In 1925 there were 26 trains on the Isle of Wight Railway 'main line' from Ryde to Ventnor daily, the average journey times varying between 48 and 53 minutes. In 1936 there were 38 such trains and timings were reduced to between 44 and 47 minutes.

Despite the limited scope for fast or non-stop running, there had been some well-meant efforts in the past. In 1891 the IWR had put on an 'Invalid Express' (four first-class coaches plus a van), 35 tons in all, for patients suffering from consumption and visiting the well-known hospital at Ventnor. It ran non-stop from Ryde Pier Head to Ventnor, $12\frac{1}{2}$ miles, in a booked time of 21 minutes, sometimes in practice reduced to $18\frac{1}{2}$ minutes. This was despite a speed restriction to 10 mph along Ryde Pier, slowing for staff exchanges at St John's Road, Sandown and Shanklin, and three miles up at 1 in 70 to Ventnor. The invalids must have been quite shaken up on occasion.

Other ventures included through trains between Ventnor and Freshwater via Newport, or Ryde and Freshwater, with limited stops. In the 1930s 'The Tourist' through train, Ventnor–Freshwater, with an improvised observation coach, was very popular with summer visitors. In the last year of the Southern's independent existence, 1947, an ex-LBSCR E4 0–6–2T was imported with the idea of speeding up the Ryde–Ventnor services; however, clearance problems on that route restricted this engine's use to the Sandown–Cowes line, where its power was not required, and it was returned to the mainland in 1948.

The St John's Road workshops of the IWR were extended to serve the Island's railway needs – a miniature Eastleigh or Ashford, in fact, though the former Newport works of the Isle of Wight Central Railway continued in existence for the painting and renovation of coaching stock. The versatility of St John's Road was shown by the construction there of a 'geared manual tractor' named 'Midget' and designed by the then Assistant for the Isle of Wight, A. B. MacLeod, in 1930, for moving wagons about the works, chiefly to save lighting up an extra engine for this purpose.

In 1933 heavy repairs were required on the Ryde Pier Head track supports. When rebuilding was carried out, the

133

opportunity was taken to put in a fourth platform to help handle the increased number of trains on the Ryde–Ventnor section.

The jointly owned passenger ships on the Portsmouth–Ryde service, five paddle-steamers in all, passed to the Southern Railway in 1923, as did the two paddle-steamers of the LSWR on the Lymington–Yarmouth route. The Southern soon replaced the Portsmouth fleet with new paddle-steamers, the *Shanklin* in 1924, the *Merstone* and *Portsdown* in 1928, followed by the larger *Whippingham* and *Southsea* in 1930, the *Sandown* in 1934 and the *Ryde* in 1937. Capacity was thus adequate for the heavy summer peak traffics, though the fleet was under-employed during the winter months.

For the Lymington route, the new paddle-steamer *Freshwater* was built in 1927. J. L. Harrington has recalled that the paddle-steamers at low water spring tides had been known to hoist a foresail to assist them round the sharp bends in the Lymington River – the last railway ships with sails! The growth of demand for car-ferry services was met by a slipway at Portsmouth (Broad Street), provided by the Portsmouth Corporation. This was matched by one at Fishbourne, near Ryde. The Southern's first car carrier was the *Fishbourne* of 1927, followed by the *Wootton* in 1928 and the *Hillsea* in 1930. A combined passenger and car ferry, the *Lymington*, was built for that service in 1938, followed in 1947 by a second, *Farringford*, named after Tennyson's former home on the island. Tennyson is reputed to have written 'Crossing the Bar' while returning to Farringford from the mainland on one of the old paddle-steamers.

The shortness of most journeys in the Isle of Wight rendered the railways very vulnerable to road competition. Dodson Bros of Newport began bus operations in 1921 and expanded steadily until in 1929 the Southern Vectic Omnibus Co. Ltd, in which the Southern Railway held a 50 per cent interest (as related in Chapter 15), was formed to take over Dodson's business, which by that time covered the principal routes in the island. However, the day when private cars and buses together would force the closure of all the island's railways apart from the Ryde–Shanklin section was never foreseen in Southern Railway days.

Chapter 15

THE SOUTHERN ON THE ROAD AND IN THE AIR

Soon after the motor bus became a reasonably reliable form of transport (and in some cases before then), several railway companies conceived an interest in operating road passenger services. The Great Western, very conservative in some aspects but surprisingly forward-thinking in others, obtained statutory road powers and inaugurated a bus service between Helston and the Lizard in Cornwall as early as 1903. Its road operations expanded until by 1927 it had 232 vehicles. This example was not followed on such a scale by any other railway, partly on account of uncertainty regarding statutory powers. Parliament, rather illogically, had granted these to the North Eastern, Great Eastern, North Staffordshire and Great North of Scotland Railways but refused them to the Great Northern, the London & South Western and the London Brighton & South Coast. To add to the confusion, several railways operated road services without any specific powers, but were not challenged, while the North Eastern Railway did not use the powers it had obtained.

The Great Western's enterprise was most marked in sparsely populated areas such as Cornwall and West Wales and it was matched by the Great North of Scotland Railway's bus activities in the north-east corner of Scotland.

The London & South Western Railway had early on operated buses from Haslemere station to Hindhead and Farnham, and between Exeter and Chagford. The Southern also inherited an historical curiosity from the SECR in the shape of a horse tramway, with toast-rack cars, between Hythe and Sandgate. It ran partly along the town streets and partly on a reserved track. It did not long survive the Grouping in 1923.

The Southern Railway was conscious of the fact that the

135

Railways Act 1921 had granted it no road powers; but it made no move to apply for them until 1928, when all four main line railways were successful in obtaining road transport powers under four Acts of Parliament, identical in wording except for the titles. The railways, meanwhile, had given the House of Commons Select Committee considering the Bills an undertaking not to obtain majority control of bus undertakings, to avert the charge of seeking monopoly power.

After the Acts were passed, a question faced the Companies. Should they start to operate buses on a large scale and enter into competition with existing services? It was arguable that this would promote local co-ordination of rail and bus services, with buses meeting trains at joint rail and bus stations, and general interavailability of tickets. And it would be relatively easy to substitute buses for trains on branch lines with very light traffic. Alternatively, should the railways merely invest in existing bus companies on a partnership basis?

The Southern's reluctance to engage in bus operation itself was emphatic; of the main line companies, it had inherited in 1923 the fewest buses from its constituents – just one vehicle. And Walker's attitude has been quoted verbatim by Sir John Elliot: 'We are not busmen and we never will be. We want to employ the professionals to run our investment'. This principle was generally accepted; even the Great Western agreed to dispose of its buses to railway-associated bus companies. The Southern began investing steadily, following a meeting on 7 November 1928 between the railways and the Tilling/British Automobile Traction group at which a negotiating committee was set up to plan the railway participation.

The patterns of organisation and ownership in the bus industry were complex and changing rapidly, following the phenomenal growth of the early 1920s. The old-established firm of Thomas Tilling, originally horse-and-cart carriers, had moved into the motor bus business and joined forces with the British Automobile Traction Company, an associate of the British Electric Traction Company which originally controlled a network of tramway systems but was moving steadily into the bus business, and which also had a close working arrangement with Thomas Tilling. Then there was the National Omnibus

136

Company, and the National Electric Construction Company (the Balfour Beatty Group), each with subsidiary operating companies. National had moved into the provinces from London, where it had for a time operated steam buses. There were also numerous independent bus companies of varying size.

By the end of 1930 the Southern Railway had acquired substantial holdings in the following companies:

> Hants & Dorset Motor Services
> Thames Valley Traction Company
> Devon General Omnibus & Touring Company
> Wilts & Dorset Motor Services
> Southern National Motor Services
> Aldershot & District Traction Company
> East Kent Road Car Company
> Maidstone & District Motor Services
> Southdown Motor Services
> Southern Vectis Motor Services

The participation in Devon General and Thames Valley was joint with the GWR. The Vectis company was a special case; the Southern Railway had bought up the bus business of Dodson Bros of Newport in its entirety and then transferred the management and half the equity to the Tilling Group, under the name of Southern Vectis.

The understanding between the main line railways and the BET and Tilling Groups was that their holdings in the operating companies should be exactly equal, however many outside independent shareholders there were; and that the chairmanships, except for Southern Vectis, should all be held by the bus side. In cases where two railway companies were interested, their combined holdings were made equal to the holdings of the BET Group, the Tilling Group, or the combined Tilling and British Automobile Traction.

Substantial minority holdings in fact existed in several companies; the capital of Southdown Motor Services was divided in approximately equal thirds between BET, the Southern Railway, and outside shareholders. Another special case was the East Surrey Traction Company, owned by the

London Underground combine. As the drafting of the London Passenger Transport Bill proceeded, it became clear that part of East Surrey's business would lie outside the statutory London Passenger Transport Area. Accordingly, the Southern Railway purchased these routes and transferred them to the Southdown Company.

The Southern Railway also obtained an interest in several long-distance coach services, jointly in some cases with the GWR, which were then transferred to bus companies associated with the railways. These included the 'Royal Blue' London–Bournemouth service. It was the coach services rather than the local country buses that caused the railways concern. The Southern Railway Chairman's speech at the Annual General Meeting in 1930 contained a rather quaintly old-fashioned reference to 'char-à-banc competition' facing the railway.

Various historians have criticised the main line railways for their bus policies. John Hibbs has written: 'The railway companies and the combine made no serious attempt to integrate their trading activities.' Some colour is given to this by Sir Herbert Walker's instructions to Elliot when the latter was about to represent the Southern on a bus board, which Elliot has quoted in his autobiography. 'When you go to a road transport board meeting, you represent our investment in that company. Remember – you do not go as a railwayman.'

On the other side, the British Railways Press Bureau published in 1930 a leaflet entitled 'Co-ordinating Rail and Road Traffic: How the Public Will Benefit'. It claimed that progress had been made towards:

Ticket interavailability,
Connecting train and bus services,
Joint timetables,
Use of buses as an extension of the railway for pleasure
    and other purposes,
Combined rail and road tours.

In fact, progress in these directions was far from spectacular. The Southern, however, was helped by its 'clock-face' time-tabling principles, which were normal in the bus world and helped to establish bus and rail connections at many points. A. F. R. Carling of the Southdown Company, for instance, was supplied with an advance copy of the new working timetable of the Brighton electrified services in 1933 and arranged to retime bus services linking Brighton Central station with outlying places such as Rottingdean in order to provide good rail and bus connections.

The Southern was also notable in that it included, in its published timetables, tables of bus connections with main line trains, especially to remote areas in the West Country, and also for the link between Southampton West and the Royal Pier, to serve the sailings of the Southampton, Isle of Wight & South of England Royal Mail Steam Packet Company to Cowes. (Surely the shipping company with the longest name on the register, almost rivalling the Swiss Vierwaldstätterseedampfschifffahrt-saktiengesellschaft!)

But even the Southern's enterprise came too late to build joint bus and railway stations. Buses tended to be based on city centres or market-places away from the railway; even where they served country districts they often ignored the branch railway stations. Standing Joint Committees of the railways and the bus companies were supposed to promote the sort of measures quoted by the British Railways Press Bureau; they were not very effective.

The Southern representatives on bus company boards in 1933 included:

Sir Francis Dent (SR Director)	1 company
G. S. Szlumper (Assistant General Manager)	8 companies
R. G. Davidson (Joint Accountant)	7 companies.

In addition, the Divisional Superintendent (Western) sat on the Devon General Board, and A. B. MacLeod sat on the Southern Vectis Board, with his special knowledge of the Isle of Wight.

Unusually, a railwayman (Szlumper) was Chairman of the Vectis Board and the Company's head office, equally unusually, was at Waterloo Station. From 1932 the Road Transport Liaison Officer at Waterloo, H. A. Short, held one directorship

139

until his appointment as Assistant Docks and Marine Manager in October 1936.

In 1930 Parliament passed the Road Traffic Act, which established road service licensing; the railways were entitled to object to the grant of licences and not infrequently did so. The main thrust of their objections was against long-distance coach services which they rightly considered potentially dangerous competitors. They objected in particular to the licensing of extra services at holiday peak periods – attracting away from the railways remunerative traffics which often involved no extra expense but merely improved the load factor on the existing train service.

On the whole, the railways were not ill satisfied with the decisions of the Traffic Commissioners. The Southern did not engage in any of the classic battles before the Commissioners which were undertaken by the Northern lines and which built up a body of case-law under the 1930 Act. Even so, it was considered appropriate for Short to be succeeded by a railway solicitor, J. C. Chambers, in 1930.

The road powers covered freight as well as passenger operations. The Southern joined the other three main lines in the purchase of Carter Paterson and – through the Hays Wharf Cartage Company – the historic carrying firm of Pickfords. The Southern was not interested, as the Northern lines were, in acquiring long-distance lorry operators, but the road powers were valuable in giving statutory authority to a certain amount of trunk motor operations between depots under regional concentration schemes, which might otherwise have been considered *ultra vires* as they exceeded the collection and delivery of rail-borne goods.

Only a year after the grant of road powers, the railways applied for and received air transport powers, again by means of four identical private Acts of Parliament. Ever since commercial civil aviation began to develop in the 1920s, the railways had taken a certain interest in the extent to which they might either participate in it, or experience competition from it. The Great Western saw scope for an air connection between Cardiff and Plymouth which would obviate using the Great Way Round via

Bristol. The London Midland & Scottish saw air services such as London–Belfast as strong potential competitors of the rail-and-sea journey, as in the case of some Anglo-Scottish services. The London & North Eastern was the least interested of the Big Four.

The Southern was in a special position. Much of its traffic was too short-distance to be vulnerable to air competition. But there was a potential threat to the Continental routes, above all London–Paris, and also to services to the Channel Islands and the Isle of Wight. Even before the grant of powers in 1929, the Southern tried to beat the starting gun by buying up shares in Imperial Airways, and it actually owned 20 per cent of the equity at the time of the Royal Assent. Negotiations then started to persuade Imperial Airways – whose chairman was the former railwayman and former Minister of Transport, Sir Eric Geddes – to sell its Paris and Brussels routes to the railway. However, terms could not be agreed and the Southern then sold its Imperial Airways shares.

In 1933 the four railway General Managers met and decided to form a joint railway airline to be called Railway Air Services. Sir Harold Hartley, a Vice-President of the LMS, was the Chairman. Railway Air Services worked in association with other companies, particularly Spartan Air Lines, which was a subsidiary of Whitehall Securities Ltd (part of the Pearson financial empire), which had other air interests. The Hon. Clive Pearson was a member of the SR Board. The organisation of RAS was basically designed to achieve rail and air co-ordination. Imperial Airways provided not only pilots but also the maintenance staff. The traffic staff at airports on the other hand were appointed by the railways, who took responsibility, either jointly or wholly, for the financial results on routes within their respective territorial areas.

A number of smaller companies had begun services within Southern Railway territory. In 1932, Portsmouth, Southsea & Isle of Wight Aviation had started a Portsmouth–Ryde–Shanklin air ferry; a Bournemouth–Shanklin–Ryde service followed. Jersey Airways opened a service (from St Helier beach) to Portsmouth which developed in 1934 into a Heston–Jersey service.

141

The Southern's own first venture was a daily service from Croydon to the Isle of Wight, starting in May 1934, in which seven passengers could be carried in a three-engined monoplane. This service was originally advertised as 'Spartan Air Lines in association with Railway Air Services' and it lasted until the outbreak of war in 1939. The Jersey Airways service was taken over by another railway subsidiary, Great Western & Southern Airlines, but only after a proper airfield became available in Jersey. (Using the beach as a landing strip had led to a fatal accident.) Great Western & Southern Airlines was formed in December 1938 out of Channel Air Ferries, a member of Captain Gordon Olley's aviation group; its services had included one from London to Le Touquet.

The first true RAS service involving the Southern was a link first between Brighton and Ryde and then from Southampton to Bristol, Birmingham and Liverpool.

It is therefore hard to argue that the Southern Railway used its air powers either inadequately or unwisely, especially in view of the very rocky economics of air transport before the Second World War. (The Southern made a typical loss in 1935 of £4,770 on its air operations.) Had it done less, it could have been accused of ignoring a potential threat; had it done much more, it could have wasted the shareholders' money.

Sir Herbert Walker was not especially air-minded. It is believed that, like Lord Stamp of the LMS, he never flew. But, just as Lord Stamp was backed up by the enthusiasm of Sir Harold Hartley, Walker had J. B. Elliot, whose interest and progressive outlook were shared by J. L. Harrington, Assistant to the Traffic Manager and later to the General Manager. Both Elliot and Harrington enjoyed a close relationship with W. P. (later Sir William) Hildred, Director-General of Civil Aviation, and later Director-General of the International Air Traffic Association in Montreal. This relationship materially assisted the Southern in those difficult formative years.

To Harrington much of the detailed work on air transport liaison was entrusted. He has recalled that at one stage the Southern Railway Board was inclined to break away from the RAS concept, and commissioned a report from consultants to report on developments in air transport affecting the Southern

Railway. The link with Spartan ended before the outbreak of war, and the Southern, apart from the war, might have 'gone it alone' in the air transport field.

In ways other than operational flying, the Southern was also air-minded. It opened in 1935 Shoreham Airport station on the site of the former Bungalow Town Halt, to serve the airport terminal building. More important for the future, Gatwick Racecourse and Tinsley Green stations on the London–Brighton main line were to acquire significance and eventually be replaced by the present Gatwick Airport station.

By 1937 Imperial Airways had decided that its long-distance Empire Air Routes should be operated with flying boats, the large Short C class, based on Southampton. Twice weekly at least, the 8.30 am from Waterloo started to convey a portion consisting of one or two Pullman cars and a brake van for Southampton Docks, with roof boards labelled 'Imperial Airways Empire Service'. The brake van housed a weighing machine in which the passengers and their luggage were weighed *en route*, and the load sheet for the flight was partly entered up. Later the service was transferred to Victoria, where platform 17 adjoined the Imperial Airways offices at which passengers could be booked in. The airline passengers then enjoyed special trains, which travelled either via Balham, Tooting and Wimbledon or via East Putney, Clapham Junction and Stewarts Lane to pass to or from the South Western main line.

The Southern's activities in the air virtually ceased at the outbreak of war. Railway Air Services came under the control of an Associated Airways Joint Committee, set up in May 1940 to operate official flights in accordance with the requirements of the Secretary of State for Air. The flying-boat service (for VIPs only during the war) was then based on Poole Harbour, but the special train service continued.

Although the Swinton Committee on the future of civil air transport later recommended that the railways should again be allowed to participate after the war, the government rejected this. The British European Airways Corporation was formed in 1946 to provide all internal and European services, and on 1 February 1947 it acquired both Railway Air Services and Great

143

Western & Southern Air Lines. Under nationalisation, which
followed eleven months later, the railways lost all their road and
air transport powers.

Chapter 16

MEALS ON WHEELS AND ELSEWHERE

Whereas the other three main line railways had substantial investments in hotels, which they usually managed directly together with their train and station catering, the Southern, whilst performing some management, also inherited a complex network of agreements with catering contractors. The London & South Western owned the South Western Hotel at Southampton, which was managed by the firm of Spiers and Pond until it was requisitioned during the 1914–18 war and turned into offices. The Junction Hotel at Eastleigh was also owned, but was managed for the railway first by Spiers and Pond and later by Frederick Hotels. The Knowle Hotel at Sidmouth in Devonshire, a post-war acquisition, was directly managed.

The London Brighton & South Coast Railway had owned but never managed the Terminus Hotel in Brighton; it was probably simply regarded as an 'estate property', and nothing to do with the station. The same railway had bought the Grosvenor Hotel adjoining Victoria Station in 1899 and leased it to Gordon Hotels for fifty years, greatly extending it when the station was reconstructed in 1907–8.

The London and Paris Hotel at Newhaven, also LBSCR-owned, was operated by another firm, Bertrams, an associate of the Aerated Bread Company which operated the chain of ABC tea shops.

From the South Eastern & Chatham Railway the Southern acquired quite substantial hotel interests. The summary of the ex-SER hotels is as follows:

London	Charing Cross Hotel	Worked by railway
London	Cannon Street Hotel	Worked by railway

London	Craven Hotel	Worked by railway
Dover	Lord Warden Hotel	Not worked
Deal	South Eastern Hotel	Worked by railway
Hythe	Imperial Hotel	Not worked
Port Victoria	Port Victoria Hotel	Not worked

The Charing Cross Hotel, successful and well regarded by its patrons, played an important role in the life of the Southern Railway. The Board of Directors dined there before Board meetings. The General Manager entertained important customers there, as did some chief officers, though the Chairman and the General Manager had their own mess in the Waterloo Station offices for lunches. The hotel's private meeting rooms were also much used for general railway business.

Strangely, the Cannon Street Hotel, which had no real competitor in the City of London apart from the LNER's Great Eastern Hotel, was not financially successful and it was sold for conversion of the bedrooms to offices in the early 1930s, though the Great and Pillar Halls continued to cater for functions.

The Port Victoria Hotel was a curiosity. It had been opened together with the railway in 1882 and lasted until 1952. Though called an hotel, it was really a refreshment room with a few bedrooms. It was a wooden structure, lit by oil lamps, and originally it had been leased to the brewers, H. & G. Simonds of Reading. In late Victorian times Port Victoria had been the favoured port for members of German royalty coming to visit Queen Victoria in the German Royal Yacht. (Queenborough, on the opposite side of the estuary, was more of a commercial success as a port, even though it lacked a wooden hotel!)

The enterprise of the former South Eastern Railway in the hotel field had not been matched by the competing Chatham Company. However, the LCDR did build a hotel at Holborn Viaduct in 1897 which was leased on the basis of a rent equal to 6 per cent of the building cost plus 10 per cent of the profits. It was unsuccessful and was converted into offices.

The expert in these complicated arrangements was Charles Sheath, the ex-SER Director who was Chairman of the SR Hotels Committee and who supported direct management, in friendly opposition to Walker's policy that, in principle, railwaymen should concentrate upon running trains and leave catering to catering experts. However, Walker qualified this by requiring that (a) railway passengers should be well served, and (b) that the Company should benefit financially, from rentals and/or a share in the contractor's takings. By and large, the Southern's relationship with its contractors was satisfactory. Frederick Hotels in particular was a very efficient organisation; it had been founded by Frederick Gordon, the founder also of Gordon Hotels, and Sir Blundell Maple, who chaired the great furniture firm and had built the Great Central Hotel in London.

The relationships covering the refreshment rooms at stations were equally complex. As a curious sidelight, it may be mentioned that an entry in the 1921 edition of *Bradshaw's Railway Manual* shows that the Buffet de la Gare in the Gare Maritime at Boulogne was owned by the South Eastern Railway Company (*not* the SECR Managing Committee).

On the South Western side the Southern's refreshment rooms were run initially by Spiers and Pond and later by Frederick Hotels. At Waterloo, Fredericks showed to advantage; the Surrey Rooms on the first floor, overlooking the station concourse, served excellent meals at reasonable prices, whilst on the ground floor the Windsor Tea Room performed the same function for lighter refreshments. The Long Bar nearby was much patronised by tired business men returning to their Surrey and Hampshire residences in the evening.

On the Brighton side, Bertrams were the contractors, except that in Victoria Station the main rooms were run in conjunction with the Grosvenor Hotel by Gordon Hotels. On the South Eastern and Chatham side, Frederick Hotels were the general contractor; but J. Lyons & Co. had a long-standing contract at Blackfriars. And at Charing Cross Station the refreshment rooms were run in conjunction with the hotel.

Catering on the ships also varied. The Southern had different arrangements at its chief marine bases. The ships based on Southampton and Lymington were directly managed. The Portsmouth–Isle of Wight service was originally provided by Portsmouth United Breweries, but later came under direct management. At Newhaven the ships were looked after by Bertrams; at Dover and Folkestone, by Fredericks. But there was an important difference in ship catering compared with train catering. In general, the caterer only supplied the food, drink and loose equipment; the provision of staff was the railway Company's responsibility.

Restaurant car contractors were not quite as numerous as those involved in station catering. Apart from the Pullman Car Company, whose range of services is described below, Spiers and Pond, and after 1 January 1931 Fredericks, had the monopoly on the South Western side. Fredericks serviced the restaurant cars from a large depot in the cellars of Waterloo Station. But, even exceeding in importance the contribution of Fredericks, there was the long-standing association of the Pullman Car Company with the Southern's predecessors, continued after 1923 in a generally harmonious working relationship. It had all started as long ago as 1875 when the LBSCR had been much impressed by the enterprise of the Midland Railway in importing Pullman cars – at first day coaches but later sleeping cars – from the USA. One of these vehicles was assembled from American components at Derby before running as a 'parlour car' on the Brighton line. It was sold after a few years, but was followed by another in 1878. Yet another car was passed around between the LBSCR and the LCDR in the early 1880s.

The real start of Pullman services in complete trains began with the 'Pullman Limited Express' of 1881 between London and Brighton. It was followed by a 'Brighton Limited' Pullman train in 1898, on Sundays only, which became a daily train in 1908 and was then renamed the 'Southern Belle'. During the 1914–18 war, with society becoming more democratic, third-class Pullman cars were introduced on the Brighton line.

Meanwhile the LBSCR had been also developing single or twin Pullman car workings in ordinary train sets, including from 1907 the 'City Limited', as well as trains to Eastbourne, Hastings, Littlehampton and Newhaven Harbour (for the Dieppe sailings).

On the South Eastern and Chatham, a short-lived 'Dover Pullman' of 1882–4 was not revived until 1910. The interim period had seen the introduction (as mentioned in Chapter 2) on both the SER and the LCDR, of 'Club Trains' for the

Continental services, staffed by the Wagons-Lits Company. They lasted only from 1888 to 1893 as they were not a financial success.

In 1910 the SECR had placed six Pullman cars in its Dover and Folkestone boat train services; they remained in use until the Second World War, with a period of withdrawal during the 1914–18 war. In 1921 a Sundays-only 'Thanet Pullman Limited' was inaugurated, for first-class passengers only, between Victoria and Ramsgate.

On the London & South Western Railway a few Pullman cars ran after 1880, on both Exeter and Bournemouth expresses; but the Pullman concept never took hold here to the extent that it did on the other future constituents of the Southern. On the contrary, Spiers and Pond were employed as contractors to operate both the restaurant and 'pantry' cars (officially, first-class kitchen brakes) built in the early part of the twentieth century by W. Panter and S. Warner for the LSWR, until they were succeeded by Frederick Hotels. Both contractors normally paid the railway a subvention of 7 per cent on sales (*not* on profits), the sort of arrangement that appealed to Walker.

After the formation of the Southern Railway, the contracts with Pullman were renewed and extended to cover several all-Pullman trains. The most noteworthy innovation on the Eastern Section was of course the Southern Railway's introduction of the all-Pullman 'Golden Arrow' in May 1929. It was intended to fight off the challenge of the air lines for the high-class business and leisure traffic between London and Paris. On the French side, a train of Pullmans (to the Continental loading gauge) was provided by the Wagons-Lits Company. Single Pullman cars were provided in the ordinary Continental expresses from Victoria. In fact, throughout on the South Eastern side as on the Brighton side, Pullman were the universal contractors on trains except for through trains to other railways, in which case the restaurant car was provided by the Southern Railway and the caterer was originally Spiers and Pond, later Fredericks.

After the Second World War some converted Pullman cars were restored to the Charing Cross–Hastings service with the words 'Refreshment Car' painted over the Pullman name, though Pullman staff still provided the service.

From the point of view of the Pullman Company the timings of the 'Arrow' – both Up and Down services – were unfortunate in that main meals were not in demand by passengers; morning coffee, or perhaps stronger drinks for passengers fearing *mal de mer*, on the way to Dover, and afternoon tea on the return journey were not very profitable, having regard to the staff and other costs involved.

On the South Western side, the Southern inaugurated the 'Bournemouth Belle' in 1931 which, together with various all-Pullman Ocean Liner Specials to Southampton, completed the story until the post-war 'Devon Belle' was introduced, with its unique observation car, in 1947. The 'Portsmouth No. 1' electrification of 1937 introduced restaurant cars staffed by Fredericks into all the express trains on the Portsmouth Direct Line via Guildford – a train every hour (with more in the peaks) offering full meal and light refreshment service in a most lavish way.

It was on the Brighton side that, in Southern days, the Pullman empire flourished most effectively. The relatively short length of most journeys here suited the Pullman principle of producing refreshments and light meals from tiny kitchens, but always with style and attractive presentation which compensated for any lack of choice. The huge 48-ton kitchen cars of the LMS were anathema to Pullman managerial thinking.

The Pullman Car Company's association with the Southern was emphasised by the siting of the General Manager's office in Hudson's Place adjoining Victoria Station. The stores were situated at Battersea, and the carriage works at Preston Park on the outskirts of Brighton, in a former LBSCR paint shop. Julian Morel, a Chief Officer of the Company for twenty-one years, recalls that all the senior Pullman officers lived on the Southern.

A tradition that started with the 'Southern Belle' in 1908 was maintained when the Brighton main line was electrified in 1933 and the first electric multiple-unit Pullman train in the world was placed in service, and soon renamed 'Brighton Belle'. However, with the later electrification schemes of the LBSCR's coastal lines, a new relationship began to emerge, under which the railway company provided the cars and Pullman provided staff, supplies and service. Single Pullman cars ran in the trains to Eastbourne, Bexhill and Hastings introduced with electrification in 1935. But, for the 'Portsmouth No. 2' electrification, Bulleid built buffet cars to his own design, operated by Pullman staff, as described in chapter 9. The financial arrangement in this case was that the Southern collected from Pullman 5 per cent of the gross takings. This compared with the 7 per cent paid by Fredericks on the South Western side.

However, ten years after Walker retired, the Southern Board began to have other ideas. On the very eve of nationalisation it was decided to look into the advantages of taking over the catering, as and when the contracts with caterers lapsed, and an Assistant to the General Manager was appointed to plan for possible changeover. Nationalisation put an end to such ideas, with the creation of a Hotels Executive entirely independent of the railway.

What sort of service did the passenger enjoy from the Southern's policy of contracting out? One must say that it was generally excellent and, above all, the standard was reliable – the secret of successful catering. The main meals served by Fredericks were perhaps not as gastronomically exciting as those in the crack streamliners of the LNER and the LMS between 1935 and 1939, but they were always very adequate. And there was throughout the Southern a lavish availability of light refreshments, whether in or from Pullman cars or SR buffet cars. Having regard to the relatively short distances involved, the passenger can be considered to have been cosseted, whilst the Railway Company enjoyed a constant income without incurring heavy investment on maintenance expenditure. The latter was in fact confined to the ROVs and the underframes of Pullman vehicles, the bodies of which, with all fittings, were maintained by Pullman at the Preston Park works. It was an example that other railways might have considered copying more widely.

Chapter 17

THE DECADE OF BULLEID

There could hardly have been a more striking contrast than that between the personalities of R. E. L. Maunsell and Oliver Bulleid. Almost the only thing they had in common was Ireland, where Maunsell started his career and Bulleid ended his. Maunsell was essentially a good administrator, planning the future workload, setting clear objectives to his design team, checking progress, and interested in the work of individuals under his control, even down to the premium apprentices. Bulleid was absorbed in his own dreams of reinventing the steam locomotive; he would walk around the workshops without speaking to anyone, and sometimes having left for a stated destination would disappear in the opposite direction.

Bulleid has been the subject of admiration as one of the last giants of steam, and of criticism as a prima donna who too often sounded a wrong note. The truth probably lies in between. But one question is, perhaps, why he was chosen to succeed Maunsell. Maunsell's health had been failing for some time before 1937, and he had been forced to delegate most of his work. However, he stayed on until Sir Herbert Walker retired in October of that year; both men probably felt it appropriate to close a chapter of Southern history together.

Bulleid was well known to the Chairman, Robert Holland Martin, and visited him in his Worcestershire home. Holland Martin was always attracted by new, original viewpoints and Bulleid could be a vivacious and interesting conversationalist when he chose. His insistence that, despite the Southern's commitment to electrification, there were still striking advances to be made in steam traction, was highly plausible. He had worked for so long in the shadow of that dominant personality Sir Nigel Gresley that he longed for the chance to exploit his

152

own novel ideas. Had Walker remained, Bulleid's exuberance would undoubtedly have been curbed; but Walker retired just a fortnight before Bulleid's appointment, warmly sponsored by Holland Martin with the Board, took effect. His salary was £3,000 p.a.

Bulleid's two years before the outbreak of war in September 1939 were largely occupied with improving the performance of the Southern's largest passenger locomotives, the Nelsons. In addition, he introduced three 0–6–0 diesel-electric shunters – basically similar to those already in use on the LMS and the GWR, which were employed at Norwood Yard. But his main thinking was directed towards more fundamental changes in the design of an express passenger locomotive to replace the Nelsons.

Air competition was being experienced to an extent that made it desirable to accelerate the boat trains. Bulleid made a number of footplate trips to Dover to see for himself the utmost of which the Nelsons were capable. The first-fruits were measures, continuing some inaugurated by Maunsell, to improve steaming. These included fitting a Kylchap exhaust, larger chimneys and new piston valves. These changes improved the running of these fine-looking locomotives enough to enable them to handle the heavy Dover boat trains with ease – provided that they had a fireman who had mastered the special firing technique which the Nelson firebox demanded, and without which steam production could fall dismally short of requirements.

But already, looking further ahead, only six months after taking office, Bulleid had obtained Board authority to build ten new main line locomotives, the design and cost not being specified. It had perhaps been easier for Bulleid to persuade Szlumper to support this project with the Board than it would have been with Walker who was so heavily committed to electrification. It was to be three years before the first engine of the batch entered service; there had been constant changes in his design instructions to the Drawing Office. Typically, Bulleid did not consult the Locomotive Running Superintendent about current needs and problems with motive power.

Many of the basic principles which Bulleid enunciated during the gestation period of the 4–6–2 Pacific class that he designed for the Southern seem unexceptional – the need for a boiler guaranteed to evaporate water at the highest rate demanded; the value of higher working pressures; the advantages of fully enclosed motion, centrally not just locally lubricated; the publicity appeal of streamlining and speed; the provision of electric lighting for headlights and in the cab. It was in the working out of these ideas that the snags appeared. Bulleid had taken the precaution of getting the civil engineer to approve the proposed axle-weights but he omitted to have the height of the coaling stages at Salisbury and Eastleigh checked and the tenders were built too high to go under them. (This communication failure was typical of Bulleid and the sort of thing upon which Walker would have come down like a ton of bricks.) Worse still, the first engine came out seven tons overweight and holes were drilled in the frames to shed metal.

The fundamental problem of the Bulleid Pacifics was probably packing too many novelties, even if each of them could be justified in theory, into a single package. Some worked well; others did not. The high boiler pressure, the thermic syphons in the firebox, and the all-welded steel firebox were successful: the engines steamed splendidly. But it may be noted that the thermic syphon was, like so many novelties in railway practice, a revamped version of an old idea – in this case, Joseph Beattie's 'water bridge' in the firebox.

The enclosed Walschaerts gear – in a miniature form, as it was put between the framing of a three-cylinder engine – operated by two chain drives with an intermediate shaft to allow for vertical axle movement on springs, might seem to be a complicated way of doing something that most other engineers would have achieved more simply and more effectively. The chains tended to stretch and/or wear, to an extent that made valve events somewhat erratic.

The oil bath (or sump) providing continuous lubrication also lubricated the track and the lineside. The steam reverser was liable to be so imprecise that on occasion a locomotive might be running forwards with the pointer indicating 'reverse'.

Building at Eastleigh did not cease even under war conditions, though the running shed was bombed, the offices destroyed and staff killed. But the needs of freight were held to have priority and only they could justify new locomotive construction. With driving wheels 6 ft 2 in. in diameter and a Pacific wheel arrangement, Bulleid's novelty could hardly escape criticism. However, it was hastily dubbed a 'mixed traffic' type and the Minister of Transport, Lt-Col. J. T. C. Moore-Brabazon, a lover of fast cars and aeroplanes, gave it the seal of Ministry approval by naming the first example 'Channel Packet' at Eastleigh works on 10 March 1941. The class was officially named 'Merchant Navy'. The origin of the name was the fertile brain of J. L. Harrington, Assistant to the General Manager, who had had strong marine associations. The name was more felicitous than the number, 21C1, which Bulleid chose without consulting the Traffic Department, who disliked it. It was supposed to be logical, being based upon axles instead of wheels, except that coupled axles were shown by letters. Typical of Bulleid, it did not quite work out, as the individual engine number within the class was shown at the end and this meant that both leading and trailing axles had to be indicated before the coupled axles – far from the simple French '231' code for a Pacific or the traditional Whyte notation which also indicated the presence or absence of leading or trailing wheels.

It was odd that an engine officially described as 'mixed traffic' appeared with a casing which Bulleid called 'air-smoothed' but other people, to his annoyance, persisted in calling 'stream-lined'. The rank and file of the Southern called them 'Packets' after the prototype.

The virtues of the Merchant Navies were as pronounced as their shortcomings. They could steam, and run fast and powerfully. One engine ran for several days, without the driver complaining, with one cylinder's valve set completely out of action. They could make light of the 'Night Ferry' job, which normally had to be double-headed. On the other hand, their unreliability in the early days was such that, as Colonel H. C. B. Rogers has recorded, 'signalmen at junction stations became accustomed to being informed that one of the 'Packets' ... would have to quit its train at their station'. A disastrous failure on an intended record-breaking publicity trip to Exeter led to the whole class being restricted to certain duties. Slipping at starting was a common fault, quite apart from the eccentric behaviour of the steam reverser. But, on a good day, they were fine performers, and in the years after nationalisation they were modified in ways that eliminated their weaknesses and built on their good qualities.

A smaller version of the Merchant Navy class was designed to have virtually universal route availability, which meant a maximum weight of 86 tons and an axle weight of 19 tons. To achieve this, the method Bulleid adopted was to scale down the boiler, firebox and cylinders but to keep virtually all the rest of the design. These engines of the West Country class, so named because they could work west of Exeter, first appeared in May 1945. They shared the virtues and most of the problems of their larger sisters. They also had 'air-smoothing' which caused them to be nicknamed 'Spam Cans'. Later examples built after this war were named the Battle of Britain class.

Bulleid's reputation for eccentricity was enhanced by his next design for the Southern, the Ugly Ducklings of the Q1 0–6–0 class. These were intended to be general workhorses for freight built on austerity lines, but their exposed chassis and oddly shaped boiler casing looked unattractive, almost grotesque. Their peculiar appearance was partly due to the boiler casing being supported by the frame independently. The tractive effort was raised compared with Maunsell's Q class, but the engines suffered from poor brakes and their enginemen insisted upon having a 'fitted head' on the freight trains they handled. The Q1s were nicknamed 'Charlies'.

Bulleid's last offering was his most original – and most criticised – design. The Traffic Department after the war needed a general-purpose engine of medium power, particularly as the veteran M7 0–4–4T engines were becoming life-expired. Bulleid conceived a machine that would unite the virtues of steam and diesel or electric traction. It should have 'total adhesion', be driven from either end and employ sleeve-valve three-cylinder propulsion, applied to two bogies. An extreme oddity consisted in the boiler being set off the centre line to enable a side corridor to be provided to link the two driving cabs – with the firing position in the middle between the boiler and the coal bunker. One side of the engine was thus lighter than the other and to correct this the corridor had to be loaded with pig iron. The sum total gave axle weights that were well outside the Engineer's limit. The flow of instructions, sometimes contradictory, from Bulleid added to the difficulty of producing this extraordinary machine.

Bulleid demanded authority to build twenty-five of the 'Leader' class, as they were named, in a submission to the General Manager dated 11 July 1946. Missenden, although cautious by temperament, was impressed by Bulleid – more than Walker would have been – and was inclined to concede this. However, a meeting was held at which G. L. Nicholson represented the Superintendent of Operation, his chief. Nicholson argued boldly that such an untried design should be confined to one prototype for testing before a batch was ordered; eventually Missenden compromised and decided to support a submission to the Board for five.

The story of the 'Leader' class really belongs to the post-nationalisation period, as the first example was completed only in June 1949. However, it may be mentioned here that trial running took place until the end of 1950, but only one engine crew (a volunteer one) was prepared to handle the locomotive owing to the intense heat in the fireman's central cab. Fireman Talbot was the sole hero prepared to endure this, and even he refused to work the engine running chimney first; it therefore had to be turned at the end of each journey, thus defeating a main object of the design.

The trials threw up a distressing list of defects too numerous to list here, contained in a long report to the Railway Executive. To make matters even worse, in comparison with a standard U class 2–6–0, the 'Leader' consumed 50·17 lb of coal per mile against 29·75 lb for the 2–6–0; water consumption was 37·78 gallons per mile against 25·44 gallons; the overall efficiency was 2·82 per cent against 4·72 per cent.

Accordingly, the nationalised Railway Executive cancelled the order on Brighton works – the cost of the prototype and the parts for the other four, to be written off, being £276,000. Undeterred, Bulleid retired from British Rail and accepted an appointment as Consulting Chief Mechanical Engineer of Coras Iompair Eirann, where he built a 'Leader' class prototype indended to burn turf instead of coal – another costly fiasco.

A much happier experiment than the ill-fated 'Leader' design was carried out by Bulleid shortly before nationalisation, when he obtained authority from the Board to build two main line diesel-electric locomotives of the 1Co–Co1 wheel arrangement. They were not delivered until after nationalistion, however, during 1950 and 1951. They were built at Ashford works, the traction components coming from English Electric, with whom the Southern had so long enjoyed a close business relationship. The horsepower was 1,750, and the engines were numbered 10201 and 10202. Performance, especially between Waterloo and Exeter Central, where for a time one engine made two return trips daily, six days a week, was considered satisfactory.

Just before nationalisation the Southern Board approved an order for a third diesel main line engine, this time to be built at Brighton works, and with power up-rated to 2,000 hp. The delays that had taken place between ordering and delivery of Nos 10201 and 10202 were even worse in this case, the locomotive not being delivered until 1954, several years after Bulleid had retired from the Southern.

Bulleid's work in the carriage-building field was also controversial. He introduced all-steel construction in the new sets for semi-fast services, which passengers contrasted unfavourably with the more solid wood-and-steel of his predecessor. They owned more to styling than common-sense passenger comfort.

For the Maidstone and Gillingham electrifications of 1938–9 Bulleid built a number of two-coach close-coupled sets coded 2 HAL (half-lavatory) which employed welded steel construction. The sides were curved to accommodate six-a-side seating – hard and uncomfortable.

This austerity contrasted with the exuberance of the 'Bognor buffet' (4 BUF) interiors (described in Chapter 9), which had perhaps looked forward to the 'tavern cars' which Bulleid designed but which were not produced until after nationalisation. The absurd fake-antique concept of the latter, including mock Tudor brickwork painted on exterior steel panels, imitation oak beams and inn signs, was widely derided, though

Missenden rather liked the cars and defended Bulleid from criticism. Bulleid also built in 1946 some new vehicles for the 'Atlantic Coast Express' in what was intended to be the standard post-war main line coach design.

From the date of Bulleid's appointment in 1937 right up to the outbreak of war, Alfred Raworth had been heavily engaged in the final extensions of the third rail on the Walker 'rolling programme' principle. The major extensions were on the Western and Eastern Sections, on the former to Reading and from Ascot to Guildford, on the latter to Gillingham and Maidstone East. The pattern was a familiar one, with trains splitting at junctions such as Ascot for two destinations, and a strict 'clock-face' timetable.

Later on, however, Bulleid and Raworth were sparring partners, in that Bulleid's 'Leader' was intended in some ways to be the answer to Raworth's DC electric locomotive, which appeared in 1942. The 'Leader' fiasco must have been a source of quiet satisfaction to Raworth, whose two prototype locomotives were performing very satisfactorily. They had been designed to be suitable for both passenger and freight work and to be immune from the danger of 'gapping'. They were numbered according to Bulleid's new notation, CC1 and CC2, and appeared successively in 1942 and 1945. They had motor-generator booster control, with axle-hung motors. The 'gapping' problem was supposedly overcome by the use of heavy fly-wheels, weighing a ton, which would have sufficient momentum to generate current enabling the locomotive to move if stalled and even to shunt a few vehicles in sidings not equipped with the third rail. (Pantographs were also fitted for use in sidings.) These engines worked, very successfully, a variety of passenger and freight trains. They were quite frequently employed on the Victoria–Newhaven boat trains.

The Southern Railway Post-War Plan of 1947 envisaged the whole of the lines south and east of the Reading–Portsmouth axis being changed to electric traction on the main routes, with subsidiary diesel traction on the branches and secondary lines. Under this, the scope for the Merchant Navies and the West Countries and the Battle of Britains would have been confined to

159

the Bournemouth and West of England routes, and their numbers would clearly be excessive. It was perhaps fortunate for Bulleid that the Railway Executive's obsession with steam policy, dictated by R. A. Riddles, postponed the execution of such drastic changes until after the 1955 Modernisation Plan.

Raworth retired in 1945, and was succeeded as Chief Electrical Engineer by C. M. Cock, who had a background in industry. Cock's stay with the Southern was short, since on nationalisation in 1948 he went to the Railway Executive, and was followed at Waterloo by S. B. Warder. Some people were astonished when, after Bulleid's departure for Ireland in 1949, Warder was designated Mechanical and Electrical Engineer of the Southern Region – a sign that the Railway Executive mentally considered the Southern to be what some scornful people in bigger railways had described it, a 'tramway'.

Chapter 18

THE SOUTHERN'S WAR

The Southern Railway showed up exceedingly well in wartime. It handled, in particular, four huge transport operations – the dispatch of the British Expeditionary Force to France in September 1939, the evacuation of school children from London in the same month, the evacuation of troops landing from Dunkirk, and the dispatch of men and materials for the 1944 invasion of France – with great efficiency. The organisation for the Dunkirk rail services, improvised at the shortest notice, was outstanding.

At the same time the Southern probably provided its passengers with a service closer to pre-war standard than any of the other main lines could manage. One reason for this, so far as the electrified area was concerned, was that fears about the special vulnerability of the electric network to bombing proved largely unfounded: the Southern engineers seemed able to replace the third rail and repair damaged power cables almost as quickly as the running rails could be restored. Another reason was that, if the 'juice' was there, the multiple-unit electric trains could run normally; they did not have to cope with the handicap of poor-quality locomotive coal and much longer and heavier trains which affected the steam services. And there was back-up from steam traction if needed; the author recalls vividly one morning after a night of heavy bombing when Victoria Station was almost entirely out of action, save for a solitary steam train. This gingerly picked its way over the river bridge and then took the old West End of London and Crystal Palace line, passing under the South Western main line, rejoining the damaged Brighton main line at Poupart's Junction. It then continued to East Croydon, from where electric services were running normally to all parts. Victoria was back in action that evening.

When, in the current phrase, 'the balloon went up', the management quickly moved into Deepdene. Other evacuation centres included Dorking North station, Elmstead Woods, Purley, and Brighton, in addition to the Divisional Offices at Woking, Redhill and Orpington. Some offices, including those of the General Manager, Secretary and Solicitor, returned to Waterloo in March 1940, as the expected intense bombing had not by then taken place.

Deepdene accommodated a large number of staff from various headquarters departments. There was accommodation in Deepdene House annexe for junior staff (typists, secretaries, chauffeurs, etc.), but most senior staff and officers rented or in some cases bought houses in the neighbourhood. Clubs or societies for recreational purposes were formed and a social life blossomed, in which John Elliot participated with his usual enthusiasm.

Missenden's rather introspective nature inhibited him from entering much into these activities; he had, moreover, perforce to spend a great deal of time on policy and inter-Company liaison matters at the Railway Executive Committee, leaving much day-to-day internal management in the hands of John Elliott as Deputy General Manager and R. M. T. Richards as Traffic Manager. He shuttled between Deepdene, Waterloo and the REC headquarters in London.

The REC had originally been set up as a consultative body of railway general managers, with a remit 'to secure that, in a national emergency, the powers and duties [of the railways] are exercised in the interests of public safety, or for maintaining supplies and services essential to the life of the community'. The Chairman was originally Sir Ralph Wedgwood, who had just retired from the LNER, together with Szlumper, Sir James Milne of the GWR, Sir William Wood of the LMS, and Frank Pick, Vice-Chairman of London Transport.

Missenden had not been associated with the preliminary planning work up to the outbreak of war, when he replaced Szlumper. His colleagues, especially after Lord Ashfield replaced Pick in the spring of 1940, were all (apart from Sir Charles Newton who replaced Wedgwood as LNER representative but not as Chairman) men of wide experience of government policy, acquainted with politicians and senior civil servants – which was something Missenden lacked, though Elliot could help him there.

On 1 September 1939 the Minister of Transport had issued the Emergency (Railway Control) Order 1939, which turned the REC from an advisory body into the Minister's executive agent 'for giving directions under this Order'. For a long time there was uncertainty about the extent of the directions that the Minister was entitled to give and this continued until clarified in December 1940 by the then Minister, Lt-Col. J. T. C. Moore-Brabazon, who stated bluntly that it meant that 'the whole detailed administration of the railways had devolved on him'.

Szlumper briefly returned to the railway field as Railway Control Officer in the Ministry of Transport between March and July 1941. The Railway Control Officer was the formal channel of communication between the Ministry and the REC. The first holder of this office had been R. H. (later Sir Reginald) Hill, a career civil servant. Relations between him and the REC had not always been the happiest. When Sir John Reith became Minister of Transport in May 1940 he became very dissatisfied with the position. He wrote in his diary on 7 June: 'spent an hour and a half at a meeting of the Railway Executive. The relationship between it and the Ministry is all wrong and should never have arisen.'

It was left for one of Reith's successors, Lord Leathers, to sort matters out in 1941 by appointing Sir Alan Anderson, a pre-war railway director, to be both Controller of Railways in the Ministry and Chairman of the REC, with Sir James Milne as Deputy Chairman. This was a much happier arrangement and friction between the Ministry and the REC diminished.

Freight movement and priorities for government traffic constituted the Committee's most pressing concerns; on the whole, the Southern's passenger traffic was left to the Southern to manage. V. M. Barrington-Ward, the laconic Chairman of the REC Superintendents' Committee, was very much a freight man and he and Missenden (perhaps on that account) got on quite well. The meetings took place in a 'bunker' in the disused Down Street station on London Transport's Piccadilly Line. Here the Committee could, in the event of heavy bombing, use canteen and improvised sleeping facilities. Constructed between the 1938 crisis and the outbreak of war, it was ready before the War Cabinet's own 'bunker' in Westminster and on occasion, when bombing was anticipated, it was temporarily used by the Cabinet.

Access was normally through an inconspicuous street door, with security checks; but during air raids the 'bunker' could be reached by train. On showing the driver an authority, a railway officer could travel in the driver's cab from the previous station, the train being momentarily stopped at the former Down Street platform to allow the passenger to alight.

Down Street was connected by telephone, via London Transport's tube tunnels, with the whole railway telephone and control network. In peacetime the Post Office normally declined to connect its own and the railway telecommunications systems, but under war conditions the isolated evacuation centres such as Deepdene House were linked up very efficiently.

Providing alternative routes in the event of heavy bomb damage was given high priority. The main cross-London freight flows were considered very vulnerable. New roundabout routes were identified and, where necessary, fresh junctions or connecting lines were built. The exchange at Reading between the GWR and the Southern was improved by a new spur line. Some traffic flowed to the SR's Central Section via Oxford, Basingstoke, Eastleigh and Chichester; and to the Eastern Section via a new connection at Staines between the GWR and SR – real Cook's tours! The Basingstoke–Reading line between Southampton and the Midlands could be relieved, if necessary, by routeing traffic via the Didcot, Newbury and Southampton, or via the Midland and South Western Junction, by Andover, Swindon and Cheltenham. Junctions at Andover (Red Posts) and near Winchester were improved, so that these straggling, formerly little-used cross-country lines could assume a new importance in wartime. Further west, the Somerset and Dorset north–south route became very significant, exchanging traffic with the Southern at Broadstone Junction and Templecombe.

The first test of the Southern's newly strengthened operating controls came with the evacuation of schoolchildren *en masse*, together with some classes of adults, from London between 1

September and 4 September 1939. Frank Pick had been responsible for the suggestion that this mass movement should be kept out of the London terminal stations and concentrated on certain London Transport and main line exchange points in the suburbs, such as Ealing Broadway, where the Great Western and the Central Line had an interchange. It was an excellent procedure which worked smoothly, one train following another with hundreds of children with their gas mask containers, and labels showing personal details and destination, slung around their necks. The Southern's main picking-up points were Wimbledon and Richmond, at both of which there was interchange with the District Line, and New Cross Gate, which was served by the Metropolitan Line.

The railways together ran no fewer than 1,577 trains (617,480 passengers) out of London. The Southern was also concerned with some smaller evacuations from other target areas – 54 trains from the Medway towns, and 172 from Southampton, Portsmouth and Gosport.

Hardly was this task completed when another major challenge faced the Southern. This was the dispatch of the BEF to France between 9 September and 5 October 1939, with 261 special trains arriving at Southampton, the principal port of embarkation. (A second contingent left between 7 January and 7 February 1940.) Southampton's needs were a major reason for the War Office's pressure to obtain Szlumper's services quickly.

Thereafter there was a pause during the 'phoney war'. Even the cross-Channel shipping services via Folkestone continued to run. The REC, expecting heavy air raids immediately war was declared, had drafted in advance emergency timetables providing only a skeleton passenger train service. This Draconian measure, imposed from 11 September 1939, caused great inconvenience and also proved unnecessary; it was relaxed by stages between October 1939 and February 1940. Start-to-stop speeds might thereafter rise to 50 mph, though the maximum speed remained 60 mph. The Southern was not greatly affected by such limits, as it had never operated very high-speed trains.

Restaurant and Pullman cars had all been withdrawn in the first emergency timetables; they were partially restored as

165

services improved. Those Pullmans that returned on the Southern had been camouflaged to some extent and of course the windows had to be obscured to maintain the night-time blackout. On 22 May 1942 the REC ordered all restaurant-car services to stop, and the Pullman cars were stored on various sidings away from target areas, individual cars being occasionally brought back for VIP special trains.

The difference between the Southern and the other railways in regard to wartime passenger services can be illustrated by a few examples. The LMS, pre-war, had reached Glasgow from London in 6½ hours by the 'Coronation Scot', and 7 hours by the 'Royal Scot'. The 1944 timetable gave a best time of 8 hours 55 minutes. The LNER, which had reached Edinburgh in 6 hours with the 'Coronation', also required 8 hours 55 minutes in wartime.

By contrast, the Southern, which had run to Brighton in 60 minutes pre-war, in 1944 managed the same timing with a few trains. To Portsmouth, the pre-war 90 minutes was stretched only to 102 minutes. This could not be quite matched by SR steam-hauled expresses, but even here the reduction in speed was less drastic than on other companies' main lines. For a time in 1940 the fastest booked run with steam in Great Britain was on the Southern on the Waterloo-Exeter route.

The 'phoney war' came to an abrupt end with the drama of Dunkirk, when the battered BEF returned in a mass shipping movement across the Channel. The railways rose to the occasion, but it fell to the Southern to be in the forefront, lifting the troops as they landed at South Coast ports and carrying them away as quickly as possible towards destinations that could only be decided after they were in transit. The operation, code-named 'Dynamo', involved the use of 186 trains provided by all the four main line railways, though the locomotive power was all Southern. The trains were run to the loading points as information of troops landing was received by telephone from the military authorities, loaded and moved on to regulating points inland, where the military would arrange with the railway their ultimate destination stations.

The Southern had been involved with the rescue from the Dunkirk beaches before the railway operation could begin.

166

Southern ships chartered by the government included *Maid of Kent, Brighton, Isle of Thanet, Isle of Guernsey, Dinard, Paris* and *Worthing* as hospital carriers, and *Normannia, Lorina, Biarritz, Canterbury, Maid of Orleans, Whitstable, Autocarrier, Hythe, Brittany, St Briac, Isle of Sark, Whippingham, Portsdown, Fishbourne, Wootton* and *Foremost II* as transports.

Off to Dunkirk they steamed, facing heavy bombing, most making several trips. The *Maid of Kent* and *Brighton* were bombed and sunk even before the 'Dynamo' move began; *Lorina, Normannia* and *Paris* were lost at Dunkirk.

The 330,000 men saved from the Dunkirk beaches left in a procession of trains: most from Dover (327 trains), others from Folkestone (64), Ramsgate (82), Margate (75). Some landings also took place at Sheerness, Newhaven, and even as far west as Southampton. 'Toby' Wheeler and Sydney Smart were in charge, with the massive burden of the ever-changing detailed arrangements falling on Smart's shoulders. Sub-control telephone points were set up at Dover Marine, Tonbridge, Ashford, Faversham, Chatham and Dartford. Empty trains were held largely on the North Kent Coast line and fed forward to Dover and Folkestone – where the Margate–Ramsgate link of 1926 proved invaluable. Redhill was the key reception point for 80 per cent of the trains from the Dover area, frequently involving an engine change and reversal; much movement onward was via Guildford and Reading. The tired and hungry troops often received their first much-needed food and drink at Headcorn or Paddock Wood stations between Ashford and Tonbridge; the platform loops here were useful, and could allow an ambulance train to overtake a troop train standing in the station. Volunteer helpers at these and numerous other stations worked magnificently to provide what was needed for the troops during the whole nine days of Operation Dynamo.

Soon after Dunkirk, daytime raiding over Britain increased, followed by the prolonged night bombing of London throughout the autumn of 1940, ending with the two mass raids of 16 April and 10 May 1941. The Southern suffered very heavily indeed; there were many individual acts of heroism. Some of these are vividly recalled in the official history of the Southern in wartime by Bernard Darwin, entitled *War on the Line*. Only a few statistics can be given here to illustrate the extent of the attacks.

All raids on central London could affect the Southern; in 1940 alone there were 414 'red' air-raid warnings and over the whole war period, 1,227. Even more warnings were given in the Folkestone district; and over 2,000 shells from long-range German guns fell in Kent. Dover Priory station and locomotive sheds were repeatedly damaged by shelling. The Southern suffered by far the heaviest toll of railwaymen killed – 300, with 1,692 injured. The total damage and delay caused by enemy action expressed as 'incidents per 100 route-miles' came to 170 (3,637 incidents in total) for the Southern; the nearest comparable figure was 33 (1,202 incidents) for the GWR. The area between Waterloo Station and Queen's Road station was recorded as the most heavily bombed in London, with 92 incidents in 1940–1.

Waterloo itself was heavily bombed. A total of over 60 bombs fell on the station and the throat area (one penetrating the Waterloo and City tube) during the war. The offices housing the General Manager's staff were completely destroyed. Cannon Street was severely damaged in the fire raid on the City of London on 29 December 1940, and again on 10 May 1941, the whole roof being shattered. The bridge was probably saved by a bomb hitting the boiler of a Schools class engine, 'St Lawrence', standing on the track.

On 16 April 1941 five SR termini were damaged and four – Waterloo, Victoria, Charing Cross and Holborn Viaduct – were all closed to traffic on the following morning.

There was air-raid damage to the Southern Divisional office at Southampton which necessitated the staff being temporarily rehoused in a specially converted train stabled at Salisbury. As a precaution – in view of the frequency of alerts at Southampton – important office files were sent to Andover each night and returned to Southampton in the morning.

Although Dover and Folkestone harbours were closed to civilian traffic after the fall of France, there was still quite a lot of work for the Dover Divisional Marine Manager's office, connected with the chartering of SR ships to the Ministry of War Transport – crewing, payment of wages, stores accounts, catering, and so on. The Divisional office was transferred for a time to Southampton; it was bombed out there and moved again, to Fullerton Junction.

One curious wartime casualty was a train service upon which the principal passenger never held a return ticket – the Necropolis Train which ran from the private funeral station adjacent to Waterloo to the London Necropolis Company's two stations in the Brookwood Cemetery, at the end of a $\frac{3}{4}$-mile single-line branch from the South Western main line at Brookwood. The Necropolis Company owned the rolling stock (hearse vans, saloons and first-class compartment vehicles), but the railway provided the locomotives and the train crews. The Necropolis station and funeral train were both destroyed by a parachute mine in May 1941. The service was never reinstated after the war.

Southern installations at Portsmouth, Southampton and Plymouth suffered heavily in the intensive raids on these towns. Portsmouth Harbour station was devastated on 10 January 1941. George Ellson received a richly deserved CBE for his exertions during the blitz. He was to retire in February 1944 and be followed by V. A. M. Robertson, Engineer-in-Chief of the LPTB.

After bombing died down, when Germany attacked Russia in 1941, things became rather more 'normal' on the Southern for a time, apart from the shelling of the Kent coast from France. Szlumper was released from War Office duties and had a brief experience as a civil servant but by April 1942 he wished to return to his substantive position at Waterloo. The Board now faced the consequences of having accepted Missenden's demand for a substantive and not an acting post, without deciding Szlumper's future at the same time. Elliot was privately consulted by the Chairman and Deputy Chairman, in particular about the feeling among the departmental officers. He felt bound to tell them that opinion was against swapping horses in mid-stream, and that Missenden's traffic background was more relevant to wartime management that Szlumper's experience. Szlumper was thus retired with a golden handshake. (Missenden acquired a knighthood in the Birthday Honours of 1944.)

R. M. T. Richards was supported as Traffic Manager towards

the end of the war by H. E. O. Wheeler as Deputy Transport Manager, W. J. England as Superintendent of Operations, Sydney Smart as Assistant Superintendent, and S. A. Fitch as Assistant for Train Services. Alan Cobb retired as Locomotive Running Superintendent in October 1944 and was succeeded by T. E. Chrimes, who, however, was designated 'Superintendent of Motive Power', and placed directly under the Superintendent of Operations instead of reporting jointly to the Traffic Manager and the Chief Mechanical Engineer.

The sudden and unexpected death of the Chairman, Robert Holland Martin, in early 1944 greatly saddened the Southern officers who knew him. An affectionate tribute was paid in the *Southern Railway Magazine*; the writer recalled 'R.H.M.'s highly individual and very likeable personality; his habit of losing all his papers (without letting that disconcert him) and the fact that he would take other people's hats and cheerfully rush off to new appointments with headgear that neither fitted nor suited him'. He was succeeded by the Deputy Chairman, Eric Gore-Browne – 'a tall, spare man, quiet and unassuming', in the classic pattern of Southern Railway Chairmen, a banker, a country landowner and an Army man. He gave up his directorship of a bank long associated with the railways, Glyn Mills & Co., in order to devote himself to the Southern.

It must, however, be said that in wartime the Chairmanship could be frustrating. The dividends were virtually fixed under the Railway Control Agreement of 1941, and, though the Board might sanction investment, every project of any size had to go to the Ministry of War Transport for final approval. The General Manager, as a member of the Railway Executive Committee, was under the authority of the Ministry more than of the Board, though he reported regularly to the Board and submitted projects to it in the first instance.

Gore-Browne, described later by his obituarist as 'generous and even prodigal of his time, and always ready to interest himself in the problems of younger people', was also very active in Church of England affairs. He was perhaps less tough in business matters than his fellow Chairmen on the other railways.

Despite his age, Holland Martin, with his usual enthusiasm, had enrolled in the Southern Railway Home Guard, in which he was No. 1. Elliot also, with his military experience in the 1914–18 war, was active in the Southern 'Dad's Army', though Missenden did not participate.

One interesting wartime development was the working from Victoria, from time to time, of special trains for Hurn Airport near Bournemouth in connection with flights arranged for VIPs on important missions. These trains were usually hauled by a Drummond T9 and consisted of two Pullmans between a couple of first-class brake vehicles. They ran via Streatham Common, Wimbledon and Basingstoke.

History repeated itself in the Warren between Folkestone and Dover, where in the 1914–18 war a landslide blocked the lines completely. In November 1939 the same happened but on a smaller scale, the line being reopened in January 1940. A further fall closed the line for over a fortnight at the end of February 1940.

As the war moved into its closing stages the Southern became heavily involved with the preparation for the invasion of Europe. To persuade the Germans that the Dover Strait was to be the invasion route, a large dummy concentration depot was built and equipped with railway sidings between Tonbridge and Ashford. Germans agents and the Luftwaffe spy planes duly reported this feature, which was made more credible by (empty) supply trains being run into the depot.

The immense build-up of material for the invasion accumulated at numerous points inland but most was destined for the Southern. New marshalling yards were built at Brockenhurst and Micheldever to help relieve Feltham and Eastleigh. Southampton, the principal port, had a concentration depot at Lockerly, near Dunbridge on the Southampton–Salisbury line, which had 15 miles of sidings and 134 covered sheds for storage of tanks, guns and ammunition. Other ports on the Southern were of course heavily engaged – Poole, Hamworthy, Lymington, Portsmouth, Littlehampton and Newhaven.

When the invasion started, Southern Railway ships took part as they had done at Dunkirk, and *Maid of Orleans* was lost through a mine. The huge flow of D-Day traffic had scarcely settled down to a steady pattern of reinforcements when the

171

Southern, like the rest of south-east England, began to experience a renewed blitz, the flying bombs and rockets. These attacks led to a second evacuation of children and mothers; the Southern this time was concerned with movements west, away from the whole target area of the south-east. In fact, trains were run direct from Kent to the West of England and South Wales. The evacuation period lasted from 7 July 1944 to the end of the month so far as special trains were concerned. By the end of the year, the movement was tending to be in the opposite direction. The railways by then had recorded 1,432 incidents due to flying bombs and rockets – the great majority being on the Southern.

The workshops (including those of the Marine Department) performed notable feats of war production. Eastleigh's contribution included aircraft components, heavy howitzers, glider components and tank components. Lancing produced glider components and gun shields. Ashford made howitzers and standard bridge units. Brighton produced tank components.

When VE day came, the railways received a message of thanks from the Prime Minister, Winston Churchill, 'for the highly efficient manner in which they have met every demand made upon them during the last four years of our desperate struggle with Nazi Germany . . . In spite of every enemy effort, the traffic has been kept moving and on behalf of the Nation I express gratitude to every railwayman.'

The Nation's gratitude, however, was short-lived; the general election which removed Winston Churchill from office even before the war with Japan had ended returned a government that saw no future for private railway companies, no matter how valiant their war effort had been.

Chapter 19

PEACE BUT NO REWARD – NATIONALISATION

After the war ended in July 1945, the railways faced two and a half years of difficulty before they were nationalised on 1 January 1948. They had been stretched to the limit to carry the heavy wartime traffics, but renewals of locomotives and rolling stock had been restricted by government order; no passenger carriages at all were built apart from those already under construction at the outbreak of war. They were not allowed to keep the extra revenue they had earned by their wartime efforts: under the Railway Control Agreement they received from the government a fixed rental in lieu of net revenue, the rental in 1941 being 67 per cent of the net revenue, 48 per cent in 1942, 41 per cent in 1943, and 48 per cent in 1944. Even repairs to war damage were held up by controls over essential supplies. As regards the arrears of maintenance, the government had acknowledged that these would eventually have to be overtaken and trust funds had been set up into which the unspent money that would be required was paid. But controls over capital investment prevented these sums being spent as contemplated and eventually the trust funds were swallowed up under nationalisation.

The main physical problems were shortage of supplies, especially coal and steel. Large locomotive coal was in very short supply and in consequence engine crews sometimes indulged in highly picturesque language about the sort of fuel with which they were expected to work long and heavy trains to a timetable. Steel supplies were rationed, which affected repairs to permanent way, and delayed relaxation of the overall 60 mph speed limit imposed in wartime.

Added to this, the winter of 1946–7 was one of exceptional

severity. Electricity power cuts were common and railway services were often interrupted by snow and ice. The government, in an attempt to conserve coal supplies, required the railways to convert a number of locomotives to burn oil fuel. This experiment was short-lived.

Having regard to the extent of war damage to which the Southern had been subjected, it was interesting that it was probably the first of the four main lines to come close to restoring pre-war standards. There were several factors in this. First of all, Walker's electrification and modernisation programmes meant that much rolling stock was, despite hard usage in wartime, comparatively young. Then, the Southern had never operated very high-speed trains, so that the 60 mph limit had not affected its timetables as much as elsewhere. Lastly, the Pullman Car Company joined enthusiastically in trying to restore pre-war standards despite continued food rationing; it added a touch of glamour to the otherwise depressing post-war railway scene.

Restoration of foreign travel was one of the longed-for benefits of peace. The first Continental boat train actually ran from Victoria on 15 January 1945, well before the war ended, for people with special permits to visit liberated Paris. This was arranged on the personal instructions of the Prime Minister, Winston Churchill. Ships had to be released by the Ministry of War Transport (the *Isle of Thanet* and the *Isle of Guernsey*) and the Newhaven–Dieppe route employed; the essential purpose was to boost French morale with a foretaste of a return to prewar conditions.

After the war had finally ended, the 'Golden Arrow' was restored to service, with fine panache, on 15 April 1946. On its first day it was hauled by 21C1 'Channel Packet' with the Union Jack and the French tricolour flying from the engine's front, while *Canterbury* provided the sea crossing. However *Invicta* (completed just after war broke out, and not yet returned to civilian duties) was soon to replace *Canterbury* as the Southern's flagship.

The 'Brighton Belle', which had been out of action since 1942, returned as a 'semi-Belle' – one 5 BEL unit coupled to a 6 PUL set in January 1946. In October 1947 it shook off its plebeian companion and ran again as a ten-coach all-Pullman train. (One of the three 'Belle' units had been damaged during an air raid while standing in Victoria Station.)

For the summer service of 1947, a new Pullman train, the 'Devon Belle', with portions for Ilfracombe and Plymouth, was instituted. It had two novel features: it did not stop at Salisbury though, in the absence of water-troughs, engines had to be changed at Wilton, the next station West of Salisbury; and it included an observation saloon (which of course had to be turned at the end of each journey) over the scenic route to Ilfracombe. The Night Ferry was restored, on 14 December 1947, just sixteen days before nationalisation.

Bulleid was busy restarting post-war carriage building as soon as government restrictions were relaxed, initially with 12 new six-car corridor sets incorporating restaurant cars, built at Lancing and Eastleigh. The underframes and bogies were the new standard he designed for the Southern. He also started to build six-a-side suburban electric stock.

Regaining the momentum of the Walker policies after the war posed a problem which led Missenden to appoint in August 1944 a committee, chaired by Raworth (who returned from retirement for this purpose), to study and report on future electrification. The Board, by minutes dated 26 March 1942, had already approved 'in principle' the completion of electrification of the Eastern and Central Sections. The remit to the Committee included electrification as far west as, and including, the line between Salisbury and Bournemouth.

With Raworth on the Committee were R. G. Davidson (Chief Accountant), V. A. M. Robertson (Chief Civil Engineer), O. V. S. Bulleid (Chief Mechanical Engineer), and R. M. T. Richards (Traffic Manager). The Secretary was S. B. Warder, before many years to become the champion of 25,000 volts AC at 50 Hz.

The Committee's report in February 1946 came down firmly in favour of extending the 600 volts direct current system and submitted alternative estimates of the cost of completing electrification of the Eastern and Central Sections, and also for the 'complete scheme' as far as Salisbury and Bournemouth. The relative estimates of first cost were £7·1 million and £10·7 million.

In October 1946 Missenden held a press conference at which

he announced that the Board had approved plans for the future, which departed slightly from the recommendations of the Raworth Committee. They included electrification of all main lines east of a line from Portsmouth to Reading, with diesel traction of freight traffic and on the subsidiary routes. The cost would be of the order of £15 million. It was to Walker that the Board had turned for advice before reaching a decision on this. Missenden, who might have felt bypassed, had any such feelings assuaged by being consulted by Walker, who had lost none of his former skill in handling such situations.

'The charming banker', as John Elliot has described the Southern's last Chairman, Gore-Browne, had, while still only Holland Martin's Deputy, taken a considerable initiative concerned with plans for the railways after the end of the war – one, moreover, that did not greatly appeal to his more conservative-minded colleagues on the Board.

On 14 April 1942 the Railway Companies Association – the body effectively run by the four Chairmen and charged with protecting the shareholders' interests – had set up a special committee under Gore-Browne's chairmanship with a remit to report on 'the post-war development of all forms of transport in the United Kingdom, having special regard to the co-ordination of rail, road, air, canal and coastwise shipping; and, in this consideration, to give special regard to private ownership in relation to public interest'.

The Gore-Browne Committee outlined certain principles upon which they were agreed and a note embodying these was sent to the four Chairmen for examination by the Boards and General Managers. The principles included continued private ownership but a complete fusion of rail and road interests under a National Transport Board, with Regional Transport Boards under it. The National Board should consist of representatives of railways and road interests and the Chairmen of the Regional Boards, with powers to add in respect of other interests.

This report was kept very much under wraps, as it was considered potentially dangerous, going too far in the direction of facilitating nationalisation at some future date. Among the few Chief Officers allowed to see it, it was commonly referred to as the 'Gorblimey Report'.

176

The Chairmen sent the report to the General Managers for comment, which came back in the shape of a statement that the General Managers' 'experience of bureaucratic control under war conditions leaves them in no doubt as to the desirability of maintaining the principle of commercial management for all forms of internal transport'. The way in which they would prefer to achieve the objectives of the Gore-Browne Report was by establishing Transport Corporations – road and rail – based on the four main line railways. A new central body should be established to raise capital and decide questions of policy affecting more than one Transport Corporation.

Even this proposal was too radical for the four Chairmen, who were by now being asked by the Minister of War Transport, Lord Leathers, for their views on post-war planning. They told the Minister that the pre-war 'Square Deal' proposals for commercial freedom should be given effect, but otherwise no very startling changes were needed. The railways, their document argued, 'should retain the ownership and manage-ment of their existing undertakings as four separate statutory entities, and that the advantages to be derived therefrom far outweigh those likely to be obtained under any form of public or quasi-public ownership'. So far as reforms were concerned, it was stated that consideration was being given to the reconstitution of the Railway Companies Association as a statutory body to deal with all inter-Company matters; joint and 'penetrating' lines might be rationalised by absorption; railways in Scotland might be unified; and other detailed improvements such as common-user of private owners' wagons were under investigation.

The Gore-Browne Report was thus quietly buried. Had nationalisation in the near future been foreseen, it might have had a better reception, as in some respects its proposals would have been more workable than the provisions of the Transport Act 1947, which created the British Transport Commission.

But there can be little doubt that Missenden, like his fellow General Managers, thought that his Deputy Chairman had stuck his neck out in the report and gone too far down the slippery slope that might lead to nationalisation.

When the Transport Bill, 1946, was published, the railways

177

were unanimous in their hostility to the nationalisation proposals. While the Bill was being drafted, Gore-Browne told the Minister, on behalf of his fellow Chairmen, that 'his criticism must be destructive' in regard to the proposed compensation terms for the shareholders. No consultation with Ministry officials on the future organisation of nationalised transport took place. At the Annual General Meetings in 1946 and 1947, Gore-Browne strongly attacked the principle of nationalisation. (This was not, however, to prevent his receiving a knighthood, which he attributed to his work for the Southern, after nationalisation had taken effect.)

Despite uncertainty regarding the future, post-war Southern progress continued. Deepdene House became the Chief Accountant's office, replacing war-damaged accommodation in London. At Woking, a Staff Training College was opened in a fine Edwardian mansion called Gorse Hill (later to become the British Transport Staff College).

Then came the surprise appointment, announced in August 1947, of Sir Eustace Missenden as Chairman of the future Railway Executive, the largest component of the vast, nationalised British Transport Commission due to appear in January 1948. Elliot became General Manager (acting) for the last months before the changeover. Missenden must have been aware that he had not been first choice for the chairmanship. It had been offered to Sir James Milne of the GWR, whose abilities were respected in Whitehall and Westminster, despite his open dislike of nationalisation. Milne would only agree to take the job on the basis of one year's trial by both sides, and if in addition he were allowed to retain some outside directorships. The Minister, Alfred Barnes, would not accept these conditions and Milne thereupon withdrew. In some ways this was a pity, since Milne would have had a much better relationship with Sir Cyril Hurcomb, nominated the Chairman of the Commission (whom he already knew well), than Missenden ever achieved. Missenden entered upon his new task without enthusiasm and with the intention of retiring before too long.

The funeral oration of the Southern Railway was spoken by John Elliot at a dinner on 31 December 1947 in the Charing Cross Hotel, attended by Directors, Chief Officers and retired

Chief Officers. Elliot referred eloquently to the railway's founding fathers. But it was sad that Sir Herbert Walker, whom Elliot described as 'still our pattern and example', had been prevented through illness from attending. He spoke of Edwin Cox, 'a giant among railwaymen'; of George Ellson, 'a man of the blitz, our tin-hat engineer'; of Alfred Raworth, 'architect of electrification'; and of Gilbert Szlumper, 'the happy Southerner'. Missenden was also of course among those thus gracefully saluted, though he was already preoccupied with the tasks of setting up the Railway Executive.

At the close of that evening, at midnight, the Southern Railway was transformed into the Southern Region of British Railways. The Southern Railway Company, however, continued to exist for a few months longer, carrying out the exchange of share certificates through the Bank of England and settling other formalities required by the Transport Act 1947 before winding-up could take place. Under Section 24 of the Transport Act 1947, the 'vested' companies were required to prove that all their property had been transferred to the British Transport Commission, that all monies in their hands had been properly distributed, and that they had entered into no agreement which the Commission might have cause to disclaim.

The Southern was the first of the four groups to prove that it had met all these legal requirements and its dissolution was gazetted by the Board of Trade on 10 June 1948. Efficient to the last!

Appendix 1:

SOUTHERN FACTS AND FIGURES

The ability to make useful statistical measurements of the Southern's progress differs considerably between the pre-war period from 1923, which ended in the summer of 1939, and the subsequent period up to nationalisation. The records are much fuller in the first case because the Railways Act 1921, which created the four main line railways, also required them to submit to the Ministry of Transport financial and statistical returns in a form prescribed by the Ministry. These were subsequently published in the annual *Railway Returns*.

The *Railway Returns* in their full form ran from 1923 to 1938. The 1939 figures would, apart from the war, have been published in the summer of 1940; but during the war no such publication was made for reasons of security; at the same time the Companies' returns were simplified in the interests of economising manpower. Publication was resumed after the war, up to nationalisation, but mainly for the railways as a whole. The detailed breakdown between the individual railways was no longer shown in such detail and some figures were not compiled at all for 1939, 1940 and 1941.

After nationalisation, although very detailed statistics for British Railways were published in the British Transport Commission's Annual Reports, no figures for individual Regions were compiled in a way that would enable valid comparisons in quantitative terms to be made between the Southern Region of BR and the former Southern Railway.

So the period between 1923 and 1938 is the only one over which really comprehensive statistical material is available. This is perhaps not a serious handicap since 1923–38 was the

54 A Bristol-built bus in a joint G.W.R./S.R. service between Radipole and Portland

55 Imperial Airways flying boat on the Empire Air Route, at the Southampton Terminal, served by the Southern Railway

56 'N' class 2-6-0 no. A820 climbing past Chipstead with an all–Pullman race special for Tattenham Corner (Pullman cars in the crimson livery used on the S.E.C.R. section only)

57 One could dine in dignity beneath this ornate ceiling in the Charing Cross Hotel

58   The 'Trianon Bar' of the 'Golden Arrow'

59   Linking London and Brighton in luxury: 5BEL unit passing Merstham

60　The first of Bulleid's 'Pacifics' 21 C1 'Channel Packet' standing at Exeter

61　The scalloped curves of the Bognor buffet cars . . .

62   ... contrasted with the austerity of Bulleid's 2 HAL 3rd class compartment for the
Maidstone/Gillingham line

63   One of the ill-fated 'tavern cars' (only colour can show the horror of the fake
brickwork painted on the outer panels)

64 The 'leader' at Lewes o
one of those disastrous test
runs

65 One of the two electric
locomotives built by Raworth

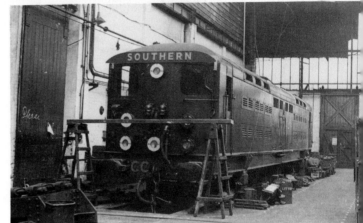

66 'Air-smoothed' (as Bulleid insisted) could look elegant – as in this picture of a Packet
2167 'Aberdeen Commonwealth' on the down 'Devon Belle' climbing Honiton bank with a
prodigious load of at least 13 Pullman cars

67 Nine Elms shed, April 1941

68 Portsmouth Harbour station after the bombing

69   Embarkation for D day, at Newhaven Harbour

70   Nationalisation in the air; this busy scene at Waterloo hardly supports Hugh Dalton's
remark in Parliament, that the State was acquiring 'a poor bag of assets'

era of major change, during which the results of Walker's policies were made most apparent.

The 1939–47 period was one of coping, with existing assets, with wartime demands and post-war shortages, right up to nationalisation. The Southern was scarcely a free agent, working to government requirements under the Control Agreement. Its ability to pay dividends to its shareholders was determined by the conditions of the Agreement.

The Walker Years

The results for 1938 are essential for comparisons, because those for 1939 are not available in such detail and were distorted by the effects of war during the last four months.

There was a minor setback in 1938 to the economic recovery from the depression of 1930–4, but in the early part of 1939, partly due to war preparations, economic activity had fully recovered.

Some important ways in which the Southern of 1938 differed from the railway of 1923 are set out below. First of all, as regards the infrastructure, the system did not change much in overall size. Closures (listed in Chapter 6) were almost balanced by new construction, such as the Allhallows-on-Sea branch: route-miles fell only from 2,194 in 1923 to 2,156 in 1938. Track-miles (excluding sidings) fell from 4,191 to 4,137.

Hotels owned fell from 10 to 8, but Company houses rose from 8,064 to 8,144 – an interesting contrast to BR's policy after nationalisation of disposing of railway houses, including those occupied by staff.

Traction showed considerably more changes: 2,258 steam locomotives in 1923 fell to 1,816 in 1938, whilst electric motor vehicles rose from 251 to 1,511. The latter number rose to 1,593 in 1939 and thereafter remained virtually static throughout the war period.

Locomotive-hauled passenger carriages were 6,959 in 1923 and only 3,618 in 1938, whereas electric passenger carriages (motor and trailer vehicles together) rose from 500 to 3,032. There was thus a net reduction in total passenger-carrying vehicles of about 12 per cent. Over the period originating passenger journeys (including those of season ticket holders) rose from 188 million to 227 million.

The wagon fleet (excluding service vehicles) fell from 35,905 in 1923 to 33,709 in 1938 – a drop of 6 per cent. But freight traffic originating showed little change – 7·4 million tons in 1923 and 7·2 million in 1938. In view of the reduction in the size of the wagon fleet, utilisation had improved.

On the passenger side the statistic of 'coaching train miles per engine hour' with steam traction rose from 9·94 to 11·31 miles; with electric traction, expressed as 'train miles per motor vehicle per hour', from 18·77 to 20·55. Electric traction efficiency also improved, when tested by 'electric car-miles per motor vehicle, per week day'; the figure here rose from 213·7 in 1923 to 252·5 in 1938.

By 1938 the Southern had come through the depression pretty well intact. Its capital expenditure had risen from £148·4 million to £173·6 million, partly as a result of electrification, purchasing new ships, building larger locomotives, and so on.

In 1923 the gross receipts from railway working were £23·8 million, and expenses £19·3 million, leaving net receipts of £4·5 million. At the bottom of the depression in 1932 the corresponding figures were £19·7 million and £16·0 million and the fall in net receipts from railway working, from £4·5 million to £3·7 million, had a serious effect upon the dividend position. Dividends on the preferred ordinary stock fell from 5 per cent to 1 per cent and on the deferred ordinary from 3½ per cent to nil in 1932.

But a good recovery had taken place by 1938. The gross receipts from railway working had risen to £22·0 million, and with working expenses kept to £17·7 million a surplus of £4·3 million, close to the 1923 figure, was achieved.

The Southern had of course, before its total net income could be calculated, to take into account its non-railway activities. In 1938 it made a small profit on its road collection and delivery services of £13,614. On shipping services there was a profit of £397,672, though in 1932 that had fallen to only £53,000. Docks, etc., showed a profit of £336,789 and railway catering (even though most of the work was carried on by contractors) a

profit of £12,400. On 'air transport', there was, as usual, a loss –
in 1938, of £4,975.

But rents from houses and lands produced £469,471.
Dividends received, including those from bus companies,
amounted to £35,152. There were other items of receipts and
expenditure before the amount actually available for appropri-
ation of £6,168,708 was reached, and of this £6,073,775 was
applied to interest and dividends on capital. In effect, all the
debentures and guaranteed and preference stocks received their
full interest or dividend. The preferred ordinary stock received
its full 5 per cent; but still nothing was paid on the deferred
ordinary stock, of which nearly £36 million was entitled to
dividend if available.

The Southern after Walker

After 1938 the Southern's record is measurable less in financial
terms than by the statistics demonstrating the volume of work
performed under government control. The financial situation
was frozen under the Railway Control Agreement. The net
revenue of the Southern was fixed at £6,607,639, the whole
gross receipts from railway working being taken into a pool by
the government, which also defrayed the expenditure, paying
the fixed net revenue to the Company as a 'rental' for the undertaking. That net revenue was the average of the three years 1935,
1936 and 1937.

The statistical performance during the war and post-war
years is interestingly comparable with pre-war performance.
The Southern handled a lot more freight during the war, as the
figures show.

Freight ton-miles in millions

1938	731
1942	1,066
1943	1,089
1944	1,129
1945	945
1946	892

On the passenger side, despite a fall during the war resulting from the 'Is your journey really necessary?' campaign, the totals were:

Journeys in millions

1938	356
1942	292
1943	335
1944	347
1945	388
1946	398

Estimated passenger-miles rose in comparison, reflecting wartime changes in length of journey.

Passenger-miles in millions

1938/39	18,993
1943	32,273
1944	32,052
1945	35,248
1946	29,231

To handle this extra traffic, the Southern's assets were virtually frozen under wartime restrictions. The total number of locomotives owned, 1,816 in 1938, was 1,870 by 1946; the operating stock (including government-owned engines) rose a little more, to 1,893. Locomotive-hauled carriages fell from 3,618 to 3,066 as no 'refreshment' of the stock took place in wartime. Electric stock was virtually unchanged. The operating stock of wagons, however, did rise somewhat to match the priority given to freight in the war, from 33,709 in 1938 to 35,321 in 1946.

Wartime overcrowding is well illustrated by the fall in coaching train mileage from 63·9 million in 1938 to 42·6 in 1941 – the lowest point of the war. It was back to 55·6 million in 1946.

The story shown by the figures reflects the rise in freight, above all just before and after the invasion of Europe. Despite the pressure on the public not to travel, apart from essential journeys, reinforced by train service reductions in 1942, the effects of evacuation and Service travel are shown in increased passenger-miles. All in all, the figures show the Southern coping with a greatly increased workload, though without any financial recompense.

Appendix 2:

THE SOUTHERN'S CONTROL ORGANISATION

The modern concept of train or traffic control had its roots before the First World War, when both the Midland and Lancashire & Yorkshire Railways introduced systems designed to monitor train running and economise in the use of locomotives, rolling stock and train crews, as well as directing action to be taken at local level wherever necessary. The North Eastern Railway followed suit soon after the end of the war.

All these systems, though their procedures varied considerably, were primarily designed to promote the efficiency of the heavy freight traffic, with its problems of fluctuating demand, use of optional paths in the timetable, correcting wagon shortages and surpluses, and so on. An important aim was to adjust staff duty rosters quickly to avoid excessive overtime. The monitoring of the passenger traffic, which was expected by and large to conform to the printed timetable, was a secondary consideration.

The Southern, essentially a passenger railway with a dense suburban traffic, obviously did not experience the same needs or problems as the northern lines serving the colliery and heavy industrial areas. It was not subject to such constant changes in demands for wagons and locomotive power. Pre-planned special traffic arrangements for bank holidays, race meetings, etc., were the responsibility of the Divisional Superintendents, inter-Divisional and inter-Company co-ordination being undertaken at headquarter level by the Superintendent of Operation. It was therefore logical that any short-notice plans, such as the design of an emergency train service following a derailment or an earth slip, should be undertaken by the Divisional special traffic sections and promulgated by telephone, or circular if time permitted.

Underlying these administrative considerations were three important factors – the high quality of pre-war local supervisors and rank-and-file staff; a general adequacy of resources, both human and material; and above all Walker's insistence that the regulation of trains at junctions and the maintenance of connections, for which there were standing instructions in some cases, were best left to the man on the ground and not referred to the Divisional office. Key signal-boxes, however, were required to initiate box-to-box messages about late running of trains.

But the onset of enemy action in the summer of 1940 and the military build-up in the South-East against invasion after Dunkirk, followed by the preparations for the Normandy invasion in 1944, transformed the Southern's peacetime traffic patterns, especially with regard to freight traffic for the armed forces. With some pressure from the Railway Executive Committee, a decision was taken in 1941/2 that the Southern should have a formal Control organisation, although from the outset the five Controls at Orpington, Redhill, Woking, Southampton and Exeter were known as Train Supervision Offices. This reflected the Walker philosophy mentioned above, together with the fact that Train Supervision Offices could be staffed by clerical grades whereas Control Offices as such required Controllers, who were entitled to higher pay scales.

Train Supervision Offices were consulted about regulation or connectional matters and did in certain circumstances give directions to signalmen or station staff who could not be aware of an incident many miles away or in another Division.

An essential feature of the Southern's Control organisation which lasted with little change until the abolition of the Southern Region's Divisions in 1984 was that it had its own independent telephone system. Selective ringing circuits were provided between the Divisional Controls and signal-boxes, station supervisors, locomotive depots, carriage sidings and marshalling yards, and an outgoing call only rang in the signal-box, for example, to which Control wanted to speak. In the reverse direction, an outlying point could only call Control and did so merely by lifting the handset. This ensured that the new system was not cluttered with normal administrative traffic and also largely reduced the near-continuous ringing which was such a feature of busy omnibus and box-to-box circuits. Direct lines were also provided to Headquarters Control at Deepdene (later Waterloo) and also to the neighbouring Divisional Controls.

The main objectives of the Southern Control system can be summarised as: to minimise the effects of late running, including adjustment to crew and passenger rolling stock workings; to design and implement emergency train services following major incidents; to arrange short-notice special freight trains and cancel trains where 'no traffic offering'; to reallocate traffic when specific yards were congested; and to monitor current performance and disseminate information about late running, incidents, etc.

In the immediate post-war period, S. W. Smart used the Southern's Control organisation as a key tool to restore performance to pre-war standards, given the problems of arrears of all aspects of engineering maintenance. At 10.45 each morning an all-line telephone conference was conducted by a senior Operating officer at Headquarters, with the Divisions usually represented by an Assistant Superintendent. Each Division's performance during the same morning's peak working up to 10.00 am was reviewed, followed by a review of the previous day's performance, with special reference to the timekeeping statistics which had been submitted. Divisions were required to state what action was being taken to prevent a recurrence of a delay the next day and in extreme cases the Headquarters officer would give instructions as to what was to be done, especially where inter-Divisional considerations arose or other departments were involved which needed to be approached at top level. Checks were made to see that any agreed action had been taken and with what result. At ground level staff quickly came to realise that delays were being pursued much more rapidly than before and by the end of 1947 the Southern was again achieving standards of performance which were not being matched on the other railways at that time of post-war difficulties.

INDEX

188